SHEILA HAYNES RAUEN

Sassy Cats
Purr-fect Craft Projects

Martingale
& COMPANY

Credits

President . . . . Nancy J. Martin
CEO . . . . Daniel J. Martin
Publisher . . . . Jane Hamada
Editorial Director . . . . Mary V. Green
Editorial Project Manager . . . . Tina Cook
Design and Production Manager . . . . Stan Green
Technical Editor . . . . Karen Soltys
Copy Editor . . . . Ellen Balstad
Decorative Art . . . . Sheila Haynes Rauen
Technical Illustrator . . . . Laurel Strand
Illustration Assistant . . . . Lisa McKenney
Photographer . . . . Brent Kane
Cover Designer . . . . Stan Green
Text Designer . . . . Trina Stahl

Sassy Cats: Purr-fect Craft Projects
© 2000 by Sheila Haynes Rauen

Martingale & Company
20205 144th Avenue NE
Woodinville, WA 98072-8478
www.martingale-pub.com

Printed in China
05 04 03 02 01   6 5 4 3 2

Mission Statement

*We are dedicated to providing quality products
and service by working together
to inspire creativity and to enrich the lives we touch.*

Rauen, Sheila Haynes.
    Sassy cats : purr-fect craft projects/Sheila Haynes Rauen.
      p. cm.
    ISBN 1-56477-328-0
    1. Handicraft. 2. Cats in art. I. Title.
TT157 .R37 2000
745.5—dc21   00-056841

Dedication

TO MY MOM, Beth White Haynes, who taught me how important it is to follow your heart, nurture a sense of humor, and keep a childlike enthusiasm for life.

Acknowledgments

I AM GRATEFUL to our Creator for the gifts and blessings he has bestowed and his constant sources of inspiration. Thank you to my mom, Beth White Haynes; my aunts, Albania and Madlyn Milani; and my almost-aunt, Wray Stevens. Our evening sewing and talking sessions taught me so much about life, love, and making stitches. Thanks to my dad, W.K. Haynes, for always believing in me. Thanks also to my husband, Larry, and our beautiful daughters, Haverly and Julie. They have taught me more than they will ever know. Thanks to my grandmother, Nettie Lee White, who dreamed quilts and made them for her family. Though we never met, her love, influence, and stitches have reached across the years. Thanks to my sisters and brother for their support and wacky senses of humor.

THANKS TO Carol Duvall for her wonderful encouragement and the opportunities she has given me over the years, and to Holly Hughes on her staff, who has been such a cheerleader and promoter.

THANKS TO the many arts and sewing teachers I have had, who showed me the possibilities with different mediums and helped me develop the skills to do good work. Thanks to my fellow artists, friends, and quilters for their love and support.

I'M ALSO grateful to the arts and crafts materials manufacturers I've worked with, for their support and the opportunities they have given me—especially Deka Paints, Bernina of America, National Nonwovens, Fairfield Processing, Sulky of America, and YLI. Finally, thanks to the fine people at Martingale & Company for their help and for the opportunity to share my knowledge and ideas with you.

CONTENTS

Projects · 37

INTRODUCTION

W ELCOME TO *Sassy Cats*! I hope you will find inspiration as well as practical information while you are here. My goal is that you will visit over and over again, finding something new each time. I want to be your cheerleader, gently pushing you along to try new techniques and new ways of thinking. We will cover several different techniques, from silk painting and machine embroidery to painting glassware and a floorcloth. I hope you are ready to learn and, more importantly, to have some fun! You don't have to be an experienced artisan. The only requirement is curiosity and a desire to learn and try new things.

Before you begin any project, read the section on each technique in the chapter "Techniques." Each section gives you an overview of the technique and tips to help ensure your understanding of each project.

Inspiration

Why Cats?

I AM often asked why cats are my favorite subjects. Anyone who has ever been owned by a cat will know the answer to this question. God really knew what he was doing when he designed these creatures. They are totally comfortable with themselves and perfectly engineered. I love to watch them. The ultimate posers and contortionists, cats just fit wherever they decide to settle in or stop for awhile. Even the most scraggly felines still have beautiful, knowing eyes. And being owned by a cat is so easy. If you have to leave for a couple of days, all you need to do is make sure the lid is up on the toilet and that there's plenty of fresh cat litter and dry cat food available. They're very self-sufficient.

In addition to being companions, my cats are wonderful studio assistants and fiber artists in their own right. They often contribute fibers to quilts or to the varnished surface of a painted piece. I used to try to remove them, but now I see the value in leaving them there.

Finally, I will let you in on a little secret. The cats featured in my work usually represent someone I know, often family members. Please don't tell anyone. This could really get me into trouble, since the cats in my designs and paintings don't always portray positive characteristics!

Childlike (or Catlike) Curiosity

ONE OF the greatest gifts from my mom was the wonderful, childlike curiosity and awe that she modeled for all five of her children. This is something we all have in the early years, but holding onto it is difficult. To keep us inspired, Mom would encourage us to explore and learn about the world around us, starting in our own backyard. For example, she would tell us that one square foot of grass was an entire microcosm of life and activity. Knowing this, we would actually sit and watch a grassy spot to see all that was going on there.

My mom was one of the best-educated women I've known, and her love of learning became contagious to her children. From her, I learned about things like color, symmetry, the characteristics of different furniture styles, and why it is better to have an uneven number of flowers in an arrangement. Even though she wasn't a college graduate (she had a full scholarship to college, but her father didn't believe that girls needed a university education), she did go to business school for a while. She had to quench her thirst for knowledge on her own. She was constantly bringing home huge stacks of books from the library on one topic after another that interested her. To this day, I also check out large stacks of books on all kinds of topics.

When I was studying for my teaching credentials, I learned a very sad thing. Most children in the adolescent years start to lose their childlike enthusiasm and give up on their artistic and creative pursuits. This is a crucial time, when they get so caught up in the end product that the joy of creating and experimenting is lost. They have a preconceived idea of how something should look. Approval from others is more important to them than their own approval of themselves. Does this sound familiar? If it does, it's time to recapture what was temporarily lost.

Getting Rid of Negativity

THE FIRST step in this process is to get into the habit of ignoring that little negative voice we all have in our heads. You know, the one who tells us we can't do something or that everyone else can do it better? I actually talk to mine now and tell her to be quiet and go away. Be careful where you do this and who is around at the time. If you're in a crowd, whisper. When you tune this negative voice out, you can focus on what your positive voice is telling you!

Filling Up!

AS A very visual person, I envision a creative journey as a constant process of "filling up" or remembering what you experience, using what you take in, and then filling up again. There are so many sources for this fuel, but you have to open your eyes and your mind, or you may miss them. Below are some of my favorite ways to fill up. All of these activities have one thing in common—they are all celebrations of life!

- ❀ Read
- ❀ Visit the children's section of the library and bookstores
- ❀ Really listen to your children, spouse, and friends
- ❀ Listen to all types of music
- ❀ Go to quilt shows, art and craft shows, museums, fabric and craft stores, home improvement stores
- ❀ Listen to quiet

- ❀ Volunteer
- ❀ Think
- ❀ Go to movies and revel at the creativity put into their creation
- ❀ Collect cool leaves and flowers
- ❀ Pay attention to your cats and dogs
- ❀ Sing
- ❀ Visit the zoo
- ❀ Dance
- ❀ Talk with friends and family
- ❀ Think about your ancestors and try to find out more about them
- ❀ Take classes and go to workshops and lectures
- ❀ Collect quotes
- ❀ Laugh

Keeping a Journal-Sketchbook

KEEPING A journal-sketchbook is very important to me. It wouldn't be possible for me to function as an artist if I didn't keep one. I recommend it to everyone, no matter what your vocation or profession. If you visit the self-help and creativity sections of your local bookstore, you will find books from other authors also expounding on the virtues of keeping a journal-sketchbook. Don't feel like a failure if you don't write in it every day or if you don't have a beautiful sketchbook with gold-trimmed pages. There really are no rules here. You don't have to write five pages a day or at a certain time each day. You can find your own comfort zone. The main thing is to just start and get into the habit of using it. If you don't know how to start, begin by jotting down what happened today and how you feel about things. If you see a picture that inspires you, cut it out and glue it in your book. Write down quotes that stir you or things that your children say. You may want to record what you accomplish, what needs to be done tomorrow or next week, or important phone numbers or addresses. These are just a few ideas. Some days my entry is totally boring and just lists what I did that day. Other days it is loaded with sketches, ideas, and notes on how great my kids are or how something made me feel. Remember that the book is for you.

Carry your journal-sketchbook with you everywhere you go. You never know when something will spring to mind. If you forget to take it with you, write on a scrap of paper or a napkin and add it to the pages later on. My family knows that they must never throw away any notes or sketches, especially if it has a little light bulb drawn on it. This means it is a good idea I want to keep. I can guarantee that your book will become a kind of friend to you. I now have several volumes and I revisit them periodically for reflection and inspiration for new designs.

Getting Started

Now it's time to cheer you on! Before you decide which project or technique to do first, I hope you will take the time to read over the chapter "Techniques," which includes basic information about all of the techniques I've used to make the projects in this book. Whether you are a painter or more of a needlework enthusiast, there is something here for you—regardless of your level of experience. Don't be afraid to try the designs in different ways. For example, if you prefer needle-turn appliqué, simply add a ¼" seam allowance to the designs and stitch them by hand. The patterns for painting may be used for appliqué, and the fabric projects may be adapted for painting projects. There are really no rules here. And besides, rules are made to break! Let's get started!

Techniques

I N THIS SECTION you'll find basic instructions and tips for doing the techniques featured in the projects in this book, as well as a discussion about the tools and supplies you'll need and how to prepare your canvas, silk, wood, glassware, or ceramic pieces before venturing on with your work.

Most of the patterns in this book will need to be enlarged to make your project. Enlargement requirements are included in the project directions so no guesswork is involved. I find that it's easiest to take the patterns to a photocopy center and ask for the specified enlargements.

Silk Painting Basics

SILK PAINTING can set you free! Before I discovered painting on silk, I always focused on drawing and oil painting. I didn't realize how easy and how much fun this technique can be until I finally bought a scarf and some silk paints. I still have that scarf and it remains one of my favorite pieces. Silk painting is a great way for children to have fun, too. My daughters have both enjoyed creating their own masterpieces in this medium. Keep in mind that painting on silk isn't an exact science. The result isn't supposed to look like a perfect, silk-screened print. The beauty is in the colors and textures you can create and the softness and feel of the fabric.

My daughter Julie was thrilled when her first silk painting, "Living in Peace," was shown on The Carol Duvall Show.

The painted silk projects in this book include "Fishful Thinking" on page 38, "Kitty Kushion" on page 43, "Angel Gabriel" on page 47, "Tube 'n Tabby" on page 52, "A Room with a Mouse" on page 56, and "Bowl Me Over" on page 61. The wooden frame on "Tube 'n Tabby" was stained with silk paint.

MATERIALS

Silk

For most silk-painting projects I recommend that beginners use 8mm or 10mm China silk, which is called *haboti.* The "mm" is the symbol for the term *mummy,* which refers to the weight and thickness of the silk. Also, white or off-white silk is used most often for these kinds of projects, and it is available by the yard as well as in pre-hemmed scarves of all sizes and other clothing items. Once you have a little experience, you can experiment with more expensive silks such as crepe de chine.

To ensure that your piece of silk is squared nicely, it is best to snip the silk, starting along the selvage edge, and then tear it rather than cut it. The silk will tear along the grain in each direction.

Stretchers

Silk needs to be stretched taut and smooth for painting, and there are a few different ways to do this. You'll need a frame in the proper size for each project. You can buy frames specifically made for silk painting, or you can improvise by using a picture frame. (Arty's, a company that sells silk and silk-related items, has an adjustable frame. See "Resources" on page 110.) Another option is to use stretcher bars, which artists use to stretch canvas. Stretcher bars are sold individually in many different lengths, and you can mix and match sizes to meet your requirements. You'll notice in the project directions that I give you stretcher-bar sizes to use based on the finished size of the project. Often, the stretcher-bar sizes I recommend are exactly the same size as the finished project. That's because the strips are about 2" wide, and they're measured along their outside edges for length. The inside of the bars will actually be a few inches smaller than the outer measurement, so don't worry—your fabric will fit the frame!

To attach silk to a frame, you will need tacks, pins, or elastic to hold it securely in place. I use Deka Silk tacks with the stretcher-bar frame. Deka Silk tacks have three prongs and don't damage the silk. Another idea comes from a friend of mine, who simply wraps a picture frame with strips of cotton fabric, mummy style. She then pins the silk to the fabric with straight pins. Elastic strips may also be used if your frame is too large for the size of your silk piece. Wrap elastic around the frame and pull it toward the silk, pinning it to the fabric with a straight pin. Repeat at 2" to 3" intervals to anchor the fabric evenly.

Silk Paints

Several different companies make silk paints. I use Deka Silk paints, which are easy to use, permanent, and fade resistant. The Deka Silk paint colors are bright and beautiful, but you can also create totally new colors by mixing the paints or by diluting them for pastel tints.

When you shop for silk paints, you'll find that silk dyes are also available. The dyes work beautifully and many purists would not use anything else, but

Wooden stretcher bars traditionally used for painting on canvas make great frames for silk painting.

Silk tacks are used to hold the silk taut on a wooden stretcher frame.

they're a little trickier and less convenient to use than silk paints. Dyes must be steamed with a special steamer to make them permanent. I prefer the ease and convenience of the silk paints, which only require pressing with a household iron for heat setting. All of the silk projects in *Sassy Cats* were made with silk paints.

Resists, Applicator Tips, and Stop-Flow Primer

Traditional silk painting involves applying resist lines, either clear or colored, and then painting the areas enclosed by these lines. Resists, which are applied to the silk with a metal applicator tip, prevent the silk paints from flowing from one area of your design to another. The finished fabric looks like batik. I use Deka Silk resists. The clear resist is rinsed out of the fabric when painting is complete, and the white of the fabric is retained wherever the clear resist was applied. Colored resists remain in the fabric.

Another wonderful option for silk painting is to use a primer to stop the flow of the silk paint. I use Deka Silk stop-flow primer for some of my more detailed paintings, such as "Bowl Me Over" on page 61 and "Room with a Mouse" on page 56. Instructions in the following sections explain how to use this material and the other products described here.

Use a metal tip on applicator bottles as shown to apply silk resist. Deka Silk paints and Deka Silk stop-flow primer are also pictured here.

PREPARATION

Washing and Ironing

I buy silk by the yard and wash it by hand or in the washer on the delicate cycle with a soap for delicate fabrics. You can also hand wash silk with mild shampoo, since silk is a natural protein like hair. Wrap the washed silk in a thirsty bath towel and roll it to remove most of the excess water. If you want, hang the silk to dry for about ten minutes; then press it while it's still damp for best results.

Cutting

Determine the size fabric you'll need for the pattern you are using. Typically you'll need to add 1" to 3" to your dimensions for projects made from silk yardage. For the projects in this book, however, I added the extra inches for you. These extra inches are especially important for projects that you'll be quilting. Fabric tends to shrink some in the quilting process. Measure the silk to the size you need, and snip the edge of the silk with scissors. Then tear from that point. Silk will tear neatly on the straight of the grain in both directions.

Stretching

You're now ready to stretch the silk onto a frame. I keep several sizes of the stretcher bars on hand, including an adjustable one. I mix and match according to the size of my project. Simply tap the bars together by hand at the corners. Line the silk up evenly over the frame and tack or pin it in place, one side at a time. You want to pull the silk taut, but don't pull so hard that the silk becomes distorted or that the tacks fly out. (This happened to me one time, and I was

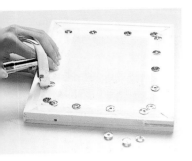

Stretching the silk

worried sick that my cat had eaten one of the tacks.) You are now ready to transfer the design onto the silk.

Preparing the Pattern

Many of the patterns in this book will need to be enlarged before you can use them. Take them to a copy center and have them enlarged by the percentage indicated in the project directions. You may need to enlarge the patterns in sections and then tape these sections together to create your full-size copies. Once your pattern is at its proper full size, place it into position beneath the silk.

"What a Good Idea!"

If you can't easily see the pattern through the silk, lightly draw the design onto the silk with a soft lead pencil. The lines will not show after you have painted your design as long as you don't make them too dark.

APPLYING RESISTS

The purpose of using resists is to prevent paint from flowing from one area of your design to another. Resists contain the paint in a specific area because the paint can't flow over resists when applied properly. Clear resist will be rinsed out after painting, revealing a white area on the fabric. Colored resists stay in the fabric and become part of your design.

When applying resists, I usually recommend working from left to right if you're right-handed and the opposite if you're left-handed to help you avoid smearing the resist with your arm or hand. There are exceptions, however. When using black resist for faces on animals or humans, I usually apply it first and allow it to dry for a while before using clear resist. This lets me maintain a nice, crisp line. It's best not to let resist lines of different colors intersect while they're wet. Allow one to dry completely before applying the other.

Shake the resist well and pierce the tip of the applicator bottle with a pin or needle. Push a fine-tip metal resist applicator onto the bottle. The tip gives you better control when applying the resist. Apply the resist by holding the bottle vertically with the tip pressed firmly against the fabric.

Gently squeeze the bottle while drawing the lines. The resist should penetrate to the other side of the fabric. If it doesn't, the paint will not stay within the desired boundaries. However, avoid a thick buildup of resist—especially the colored resists, since the colored resists won't wash out. After applying all the resist, allow it to dry for one hour before applying paint.

"What a Good Idea!"

Always practice any new technique before beginning a project. You might want to keep a small piece of silk stretched on a spare set of stretcher bars so that it's always ready for you to test out resists, paints, and Deka Silk stop-flow primer.

PAINTING THE SILK

You can apply paints directly from the bottle, mix them to create new colors, or dilute them with water to create pastel tints. Save any mixed colors or pastels for later use on other projects. The canisters from 35 millimeter rolls of film make great containers for mixing and storing silk paints.

Watercolor brushes, particularly bamboo brushes, work best for silk painting. I recommend a variety of sizes of round and flat brushes. Shake or stir paints before using them. Apply paint sparingly to the center of the areas outlined with resist. The fabric will absorb the paint from the brush. Carefully guide the paint toward the resist lines rather than make multiple brush strokes. For large areas of color, apply the paint with a foam brush or large watercolor brush, and work quickly with overlapping strokes.

"What a Good Idea!"

Watercolor artists often sprinkle salt on their wet paintings to create interesting textures. Salt absorbs some of the paint, creating a mottled or starburst effect. This same technique can also be used when painting silk. Although I didn't use the salt technique in the projects in this book, it is a fun technique you may want to try.

Simply sprinkle Deka Silk salt, which has a coarse grain (or table salt for a more delicate pattern), over painted areas to create texture. You must sprinkle on the salt within one minute of applying the paint. Allow the salt to dry before brushing it off the fabric.

STOP-FLOW PRIMER METHOD

When silk is primed with liquid Deka Silk stop-flow primer, the paints will hold their line without spreading to other areas. It's a wonderful technique for silk painting because it lets you create tiny, delicate lines—something that's hard to do with resist. People are always amazed with the results when I demonstrate the stop-flow primer method.

Stir the Deka Silk stop-flow primer and apply an even coat to the stretched silk. One coat works on thinner-weight silks, but two or more coats may be required for thicker silks. I like to use a foam brush or an Oriental Hake water-color brush, which is a flat brush, for this job. For either type of brush, a 1" or 1½" width will work fine. I recommend that you test the primed fabric to determine if it may need another coat before you jump in and start painting your entire design. Allow the primer to dry thoroughly between coats, which should take about one hour, and before painting. If you touch the silk and it feels cool, that means it's probably a little damp and you'll have to give it more drying time.

When the silk is completely dry, place the pattern underneath the silk and trace the design on the fabric with a soft pencil. Paint the design in your desired colors with the appropriate-size brush for the area being painted. Be aware that you need to let one area of color dry before applying any additional colors next to it; otherwise, the colors will bleed into one another. Also, the primer does have an effect on the hand, or softness, of the silk. It actually seems to stabilize the silk, which is good if you're making a quilt or home decor project.

HEAT SETTING AND CARE OF PAINTED SILK

Wait twenty-four to forty-eight hours for the paint and resist to cure. If you have used any of the colored resists, you should wait for at least forty-eight hours before heat setting. The silk can be removed from the frame as soon as it is dry.

Following the paint manufacturer's directions, heat-set the paints with an iron. Always press from the back of the silk with a pressing cloth over your work. Then place the silk in a sink or bowl to soak. The clear resist will rinse away in the water, leaving white lines where it was applied. The colored resists will remain in the fabric. Rinse the silk thoroughly. Then very gently, squeeze out the excess water. Roll the silk flat in a bath towel to remove additional water. Press it again, using a press cloth as before. The silk is now hand or machine washable and dry cleanable.

Occasionally painted silk may feel a bit stiff. If this occurs, you can rinse the silk in a solution of water and fabric softener. If you prefer, you can also purchase products made specifically for softening painted silk. Follow the manufacturer's instructions for the product you choose.

USING AND STABILIZING YOUR PAINTED SILK

Painted silk can be used in so many different ways. Scarves, clothing, wall hangings, pillows, lamp shades, soft jewelry, and dolls are favorite projects for silk painters. Except for scarves and some clothing, it is best to line silk to give it more stability and body. This is especially true when making pillows, wall hangings, or other home decor projects. For example, when making a pillow, it is best that the fabrics on the front and the back of the pillow be of similar weight. For "Kitty Kushion" on page 43, I lined the silk and quilted it with a layer of batting and lightweight muslin, which gives the pillow front a similar weight to the cotton-velveteen backing. "Angel Gabriel" on page 47 is stabilized with medium-weight muslin, which was basted to the back of the silk with a basting spray. If you use a basting spray, be sure to read the directions well. These adhesive sprays generally will hold for two to five days only. I have a friend who didn't read this and had a project fall apart several days after she put it together.

Appliqué Techniques for Felt and Cotton

APPLIQUÉ IS another great way to create unique designs on fabric. And appliqué isn't just for cotton and quilts! I love the look and feel of wool felt. National Nonwovens manufactures beautiful wool-blend felt in a wide range of colors.

The appliqué projects in this book include the "Cat and Mouse Table Runner" on page 66; "Feline Friend," the wool-felt wall hanging on page 72; and the wool-felt purse, "Posy Purr-se," on page 78. All three projects were created with the fusible appliqué technique.

CHOOSING A FUSIBLE WEB

Before choosing a fusible web for your project, read the information on the package or bolt at the fabric or craft store. Some fusible webs can be washed and dry cleaned. Others can only be washed. Another consideration is the weight or thickness of the fusible web. I had a terrible time with one of my early projects because I used a heavy-duty fusible web and it kept gumming up my sewing-machine needle. I had to abandon the whole project and start over. Since the projects in this book are machine embroidered or quilted, choose a fusible web that is labeled "lightweight" or "sewable" and you won't experience that problem.

I usually use a lightweight fusible web such as Aleene's. I also like Steam-A-Seam 2, especially for my felt projects. Because Steam-A-Seam 2 is sticky even before pressing it with an iron, you can pull off the paper backing from one side and rub the fusible web onto the back of your fabric. You can then draw the shape on the remaining paper backing, cut out the design, and place the appliqué into position. If you don't like where you place the appliqué, you can peel it off and reposition it before you adhere it permanently with your iron.

Always follow the manufacturer's directions when using fusible webs. Don't overheat, especially when first applying it to the wrong side of your appliqué fabric. Overheating can make it difficult to remove the paper backing before pressing the shapes in place. If you find that it is difficult to remove the paper, crease the fabric with your hand, insert a straight pin along the crease line, and tear a slit in the paper to make it easier to pull away the paper.

NOTE: *If you prefer doing needle-turn appliqué, simply add a ¼" seam allowance to the patterns and create the projects with cotton fabrics. I have primarily used solid fabrics and then embellished them by machine. You may decide to use different colors and prints or use hand embroidery with threads, ribbons, or beads to enhance them.*

PREPARING YOUR FABRICS

For appliqué projects, prepare a master pattern of the entire design on tracing paper to be used as an overlay for proper positioning of all parts of the image. If necessary, enlarge the pattern on a photocopier according to the directions in the project before transferring the pattern to tracing paper. Clear mylar also makes a wonderful overlay material. You can draw the design with a permanent pen such as a Micron Pigma or Sharpie. I discovered this when watching my friend, Debi Anderson, of The Picket Fence (a quilt pattern company). She uses a portable ironing pad to pin her mylar overlays into position. She then places each appliqué piece under the overlay, checks for correct positioning, and then lifts up the overlay and presses each piece into place (see fig. 1).

NOTE: *It is very important to keep the iron away from the mylar. A hot iron will melt the mylar.*

Slide appliqué shapes under the overlay to place them on the background.

Fig. 1

For "Posy Purr-se," you'll need a heat-transfer pencil to transfer the purse patterns onto your wool fabric. Choose a color that will show up on your wool, and use it to trace the pattern onto paper. Then you can press the pattern onto the wool and cut out each pattern piece along the cutting lines.

To prepare the fusible web for appliqué, first decide which pattern pieces you'll cut from each fabric you are using. Then trace the pattern pieces in reverse onto the paper backing of the fusible web. You must draw the pattern pieces in reverse because the fusible web is first ironed onto the back of the fabric. To trace the pattern pieces in reverse, turn the pattern over and trace from the wrong side. If you can't see the pattern well enough, darken the pattern with a black, permanent felt-tip marker. Cut around each fusible-web pattern piece, adding ¼" to ½" to all sides of the piece. Press each fusible-web piece onto the back of the appropriate fabric (see fig. 2). After the fusible web has cooled, cut out the shapes on the drawn pattern lines. Remove the paper backing and set each piece aside until you're ready to assemble the project.

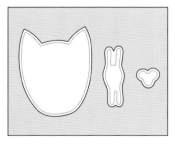

Fig. 2

APPLIQUÉING THE DESIGN

Cut the background fabric to the size specified in the project directions. Using the overlay as a guide, position each design element, working from background to foreground. I recommend doing a practice layout before pressing anything down, taking a few minutes to consider which pieces need to overlap. Then follow the manufacturer's directions for pressing the fabrics into position.

Appliquéing with Decorative Machine Stitches

Though I do enjoy doing hand embroidery, I am fascinated with using my sewing machine as a creative tool. I waited way too long to try one of the new "miracle machines," and now that I have one it's difficult to keep me away from it. For appliqué, I enjoy outlining the shapes with a satin (zigzag) stitch, blanket stitch, or one of the variations of the feather stitch. Each of these stitches is shown in figure 3 at right. Fuse all of the pieces into position with fusible web before you outline them.

For any of these stitches, position your work under the presser foot so that the left swing position of the needle will stitch into the appliqué and the right swing position will stitch into the background fabric just at the edge of the appliqué piece (see fig. 4). I recommend using an open-toe presser foot for these stitches.

When stitching around curves, keep the needle in the fabric and lift the presser foot to turn the fabric slightly after every few stitches. To turn corners, leave the needle in the left swing position so that it is in the appliqué, lift the presser foot, turn the fabric, reposition the needle, and lower the presser foot so that you are ready to start sewing the next side of the appliqué piece.

Appliquéing with Hand-Stitching Techniques

You may choose to appliqué and embellish by hand. If you're appliquéing cottons, two strands of embroidery floss work fine. You can use either contrasting or coordinating colors, depending on the look you want. For wool felt appliqués, use more strands of floss because the fabric is bulkier. Or, for a fuller look, use pearl cotton. Pearl cotton strands are twisted together so the thread appears round, not flat, as with floss.

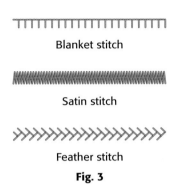

Blanket stitch

Satin stitch

Feather stitch

Fig. 3

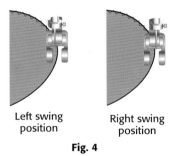

Left swing
position

Right swing
position

Fig. 4

EMBROIDERY STITCHES

The following embroidery stitches are commonly used to anchor and decorate appliquéd fabrics.

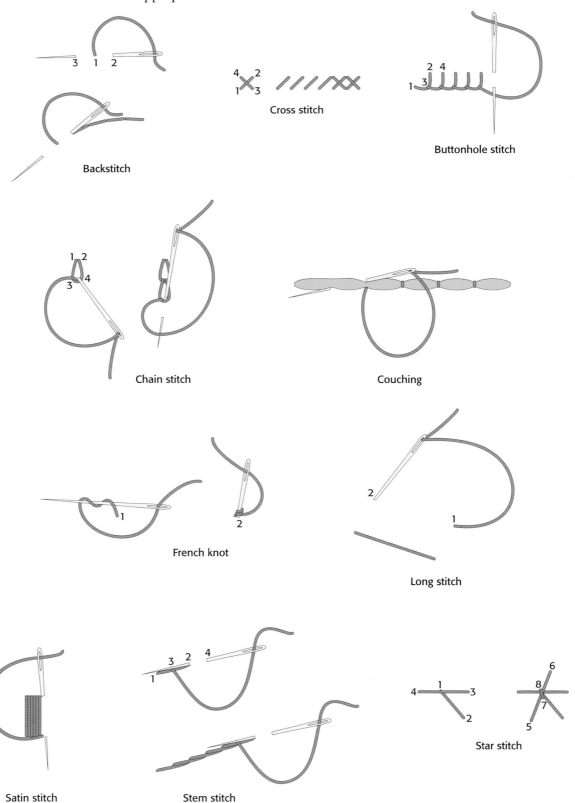

Cross stitch

Buttonhole stitch

Backstitch

Chain stitch

Couching

French knot

Long stitch

Satin stitch

Stem stitch

Star stitch

Embellishing with Free-Motion Embroidery and Quilting

ONE OF my favorite things to do is to embellish, shade, and create new colors and textures on fabric with free-motion machine embroidery. It's such fun to create your own custom fabrics this way. I prefer to use some of the new machine embroidery threads for appliqué. Sulky of America, YLI, and Madeira are some of the leaders in manufacturing beautiful threads for machine and handwork today. I hope you will enjoy experimenting with different stitches and threads to anchor your fabrics and create different textures and embellishments.

I know that free-motion embroidery may strike fear into the hearts of the uninitiated. I count myself as a former member of this group, but thank heavens I'm not anymore. It is now one of the most important techniques in my repertoire. I admit that it takes a little practice, but it is much easier than you may think. Besides, it's fun, fun, fun! Another plus is that you can cover up a multitude of sins with thread, especially if you are embellishing a silk painting with some goofs on it.

Free-motion embroidery is a machine stitching technique that allows you to move the fabric freely under the darning foot of the sewing machine. Because the feed dogs are lowered or covered, the stitch length and direction is determined by how fast and in which direction you move the fabric. I think of it as drawing or painting with thread.

Some of you may think that you need a fancy sewing machine for this technique, but there are only two machine requirements. First, you must be able to cover or drop the feed dogs on your machine so that you can control the speed and direction of the stitching. Second, you will need a darning foot (see fig. 5). I prefer the type with a clear plastic ring that touches the fabric. It bounces as you sew, freeing the fabric for you to control.

Several projects in this book incorporate free-motion embroidery, quilting, or both. They include "A Room with a Mouse" on page 56, "Bowl Me Over" on page 61, "Cat and Mouse Table Runner" on page 66, "Feline Friend" on page 72, and "Posy Purr-se" on page 78.

Darning foot

Fig. 5

SEWING-MACHINE MAINTENANCE

Before we get into stitching, let's talk briefly about your sewing machine. I must confess that I used to be very neglectful when it came to sewing-machine maintenance. Now that I have a wonderful, new, state-of-the-art machine, its care and feeding are top priorities. (I'm sure you are thinking that there's nothing like a reformed sewing-machine abuser.) It really does pay off if you keep your machine clean, oiled, and maintained as recommended in the manual.

It's a good idea to get into the habit of cleaning and oiling your machine after every project. In addition to maintenance, it's also very important to use the proper needles and good-quality threads for the top and the bobbin. I only buy good-quality needles and threads now. If you are putting so much time and effort into a project, it's worth it to spend a little extra. I'm always on the lookout for coupons and discounts offered at fabric stores. If you sign up on the mailing lists of fabric stores, you will often receive mailings with information on sales and coupons. You can easily save 30 percent to 50 percent on needles, threads, and other notions. Stock up and you'll be ready for any project.

Needles

I choose needles according to the thread and the technique that I'll be using. I use universal needles for general sewing and construction of clothing. Embroidery needles are great for decorative stitches, free-motion embroidery, and quilting, because they have a longer groove in the needle to accommodate specialty threads. If you use metallic threads, use metallic needles or you'll suffer through endless thread breakages.

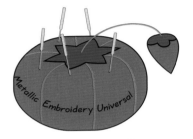

The average life of a sewing-machine needle is approximately eight hours. This doesn't sound like much time, but the needles do take a lot of pounding and abuse. If you try to get more mileage out of a needle, you'll find that your sewing is prone to skipped stitches and broken threads. I don't actually have a time clock for each needle I use, but I try to be aware of how long I use them.

Keep a separate pin cushion for machine needles. Label each section to organize your needles.

Fig. 6

In addition to changing needles after they're "used up," I find myself changing the type of needle quite often. Since I switch from metallic to embroidery to universal threads, I keep a pin cushion with a section labeled for each kind of needle. If I've only used a metallic needle for an hour or so, I stick it in the pincushion for safekeeping until I need it again. The pincushion storage is helpful because you can't always tell the different types of needles apart (see fig. 6).

Threads

I use good-quality decorative threads from YLI, Sulky of America, and Madeira for machine embroidery and quilting. I use white or black lingerie thread from YLI in my bobbin. This type of thread is lighter weight, so it fills up the bobbin nicely, and I don't have to refill as often as with some other threads. Black and white work very well with most any color of top thread as long as the tension on the machine is balanced properly. If you're working on a project that will also be seen from the back, however, it's a good idea to use the same thread in the bobbin as you use for the top.

Try a variety of threads, from metallic to rayon and heavy cotton, to create all sorts of detail on your painted silk or appliqué projects.

Stabilizers

When embroidering or quilting by machine, it's important to stabilize the fabric. Stabilizers can be anything, from muslin or fusible batting to interfacings or one of the many stabilizers on the market. Some stabilizers are iron-on; others can be spray-basted, pinned, or stitched in place. I often use a layer of low-loft batting with muslin underneath to stabilize my fabrics, especially silks and cottons. I usually just hold the layers together with straight pins. I prefer the long, sharp pins with pearl beads on the ends. They are a good length and pretty to look at. A combination of spray basting and pins also works well. If you use a basting spray, always read the instructions for safety information. When working with painted silk, I spray the batting or backing fabric instead of the silk. Keep in mind that most basting sprays will only hold for two to five days. I don't usually baste with thread because it gets caught in the decorative stitching and is hard to remove.

When a human face is part of the design, I usually do all the decorative stitching on it before cutting it out and appliquéing it to the background fabric. This helps ensure that the face will appear smooth because you avoid the distortion that occurs when you stitch through several layers of fabric. Embroidering first is especially important if the embellishing includes quilting with a layer of batting.

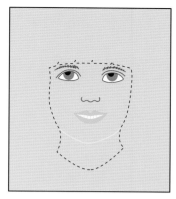

Embroider facial features prior to layering and quilting to avoid distortion.

Fig. 7

TO HOOP OR NOT TO HOOP

The more I do machine embroidery, the less I seem to need a hoop. It was very important when I first started, and it is more of a concern when you are working with silks or other lightweight fabrics. Even if you use a hoop, you still need to stabilize the fabric, as discussed earlier. I often have three layers in a hoop, including the top fabric, a low-loft batting, and a lightweight backing fabric.

Several different types of hoops are available for use with a sewing machine. Wooden hoops that look like regular embroidery hoops work well. They are thinner in width than a traditional hoop, so they fit easily under the needle. It is important not to place the fabric in the hoop for machine embroidery the same way that you would for hand embroidery. You need the fabric to lie flat on the work surface. To do this, place the outer ring flat on the table. Then position the fabric over this hoop. Insert the inner ring over the top of the fabric, smooth the fabric that's within the hoop, and tighten the tension screw.

You can also use a plastic spring hoop, which has an inner metal ring that fits in a groove in the outer ring. To install the fabric, remove the inner ring and place the fabric over the outer ring. Squeeze the metal inner ring and place it over the fabric, releasing the handles to fit into the groove of the plastic outer ring. You cannot adjust the tension on the spring rods, but these hoops work well for many projects. I use 6"- and 8"-diameter hoops most often. If you use a larger hoop, it may be difficult or impossible to maneuver within the boundaries of your machine's sewing surface.

You can use a wooden or plastic hoop to hold your fabric taut while adding embroidery details.

GET READY, SET, SEW!

Now that you have your darning foot installed and the feed dogs are dropped or covered, it's time to start sewing. Set your machine for a straight stitch. Later on, you may want to try free-motion work with a zigzag setting for different effects. Make sure that you have an embroidery needle threaded with decorative embroidery thread on top and bobbin thread in the bobbin. I recommend that you prepare a piece of fabric and stabilizer in a hoop for a practice session. You may decide to include a layer of batting in the middle of the fabric and a backing fabric of muslin for another practice piece to get a feel for free-motion quilting. Practicing first helps you adjust the thread tension so the bobbin thread isn't pulling up on the top of your project. It also helps you get the feel of moving the fabric around yourself instead of having the machine do it.

Practice Makes Perfect

This old adage is true! Practice really does help you perfect your style, and there are a couple of good ways to make the most of your practice session. Use a fabric with printed motifs as the top fabric and practice outlining the design in the fabric. Draw shapes, letters, and spirals on a plain piece of fabric with a permanent marker or quilt marking pencil, and practice outlining them. I usually go over a smaller design motif two to three times to make it more lasting, and I begin and end with a few backstitches. Writing your name and other words in cursive is another excellent exercise.

When you first begin free-motion embroidery, take one stitch; then pull up the bobbin thread. Hold both thread tails in your hand and take two or three stitches in place. Then cut both thread tails off next to the fabric with appliqué scissors (see page 27) to prevent you from stitching over them or getting them tangled up in the needle.

Now you're ready to stitch. Experiment with different speeds—both the machine speed and how fast or slow you move your fabric by hand—until you become more comfortable with the technique. I work more efficiently when I use a fairly high speed while moving the fabric more slowly. If the machine speed is too slow and you move your fabric quickly, you'll end up with very big surface stitches. Conversely, if you stitch too quickly and don't move the fabric very much, your stitches will be very tiny. Strive for even, well-spaced stitches.

Be Kind to Yourself

As with any repetitive technique, it is important to consider ways to maintain physical comfort and health. Invest in a comfortable, adjustable chair and a good lamp. I have one of the true-color Ott Lights in the floor model and it is amazing how wonderful it is to be able to see what I'm doing!

Another wonderful thing I've discovered is how helpful it is to have a pair of Quilter's Gloves. I recently found some from Timid Thimble Creations (see "Resources" on page 110).

Draw shapes and write your name or sentiments on scrap fabric to practice your free-motion stitching.

The gloves from Timid Thimble have little no-skid pads on the palms. You don't have to put as much pressure on the fabric as you do free-motion embroidery and machine quilting. This means less trauma or strain is placed on your neck and shoulders because you don't have to push down so hard. Another perk is that these gloves will help keep you warm when working in the winter. My gloves are cotton knit, so they aren't too hot to wear in the summer, either. Hats off to the genius who thought of these!

Appliqué scissors have also made my life easier now that I am doing so much free-motion embroidery and appliqué. These scissors help you avoid costly accidents when trimming threads or fabrics from your projects because one blade has a protective bill that won't let you accidentally snip into your work. Don't use them for anything else. My family knows which scissors are off limits because I label them.

I know how it is to get so wrapped up in what you are doing that you don't eat, drink, or take breaks, but this can really take a toll on your body. Remind yourself to take frequent breaks—set a timer if you have to! Take a walk around the house or outside. Dance around the room to some of your favorite music. Don't put off your lunch break until three o'clock. Your body will thank you for it.

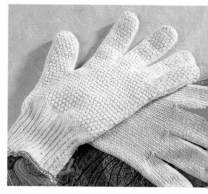

The rubber dots on the palms and fingers of Quilter's Gloves from Timid Thimble help reduce neck and back strain when doing machine quilting and free-motion embroidery because they let you move the fabric around much more easily.

FINISHING TECHNIQUES

When it comes to embellished fabrics, there's really no limit to the things you can make. Some possibilities include wall hangings, quilts, clothing, pillows, dolls, soft jewelry, cards, and framed art. The following sections describe techniques you can use to create a finished project.

Borders

For a quilt or wall hanging, making a fabric border to frame the design can add greatly to the beauty of the piece.

1. Determine how wide you want the borders to be. Add 1" to the width of the border strips for seam allowances. For example, if you want a 3" border, cut your fabric strips 4" wide. This allows for ½" seams on each side of the border.

2. To determine how long to cut your side border strips, measure the length of your wall hanging. Cut two border strips to this length (see fig. 8), and pin them to the sides of the quilt. If your center design piece is already quilted, cut strips of batting that are the same size as your border strips. Use the same batting for the borders that you use for the center of the design. Stitch the borders and/or batting in place with a ½" seam allowance. Trim the batting from the seam allowance and press the seams toward the border fabric.

3. After the side borders are attached, measure the width of the wall hanging (see fig. 9). Cut two more border strips to this length for the top and bottom of your project. Again, add batting to the back of the borders if your wall

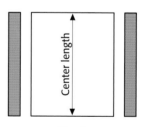

Fig. 8

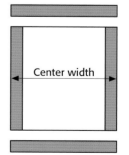

Fig. 9

hanging has been quilted. Pin the top and bottom borders to your project and stitch them in place with a ½" seam allowance. Press the seams toward the borders.

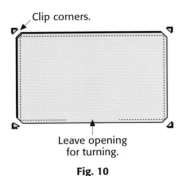

Clip corners.

Leave opening
for turning.

Fig. 10

Quilt Backing

Cut a piece of backing fabric to fit the entire piece. With right sides together, stitch the backing fabric to the quilt top, starting at the bottom of the piece. Backstitch; then stitch around the project with a ½" seam allowance. Leave an opening for turning, and backstitch where you stop so that the stitches won't pop open when you turn the quilt right side out. The size of the opening depends on the size and thickness of the project. It's a good idea to reinforce the stitching at the corners, too. Trim the corners diagonally and clip any curves if your border happens to be curved. Turn the project right side out and press. Slipstitch the opening closed by hand (see fig. 10).

Hanging Your Art

The simplest way to hang a small wall hanging is to sew small curtain rings to the two top corners. Depending on the width of the quilt, you may want to add one or more rings between the corners.

Another way to hang your quilt is to stitch a hanging sleeve to the back. The width of the casing or sleeve would depend on the type of rod used to hang it. If you plan to enter your quilt in a competition, check the contest guidelines on hanging sleeve sizes first.

To make a hanging sleeve, cut a strip of muslin or backing fabric that is the same width as your project and twice as wide as you want your finished sleeve to be, plus ½" for seam allowances. Turn under the raw edges on the short ends of the strip, and stitch in place for hems. Fold the fabric in half lengthwise with *wrong sides* together and stitch a ¼" seam. Press the hanging sleeve so that the seam is centered along one side. Pin the sleeve to the top edge of the back of your wallhanging and slipstitch in place along both long edges of the casing. Be careful not to stitch through to the front of your project where the stitches will show (see fig. 11).

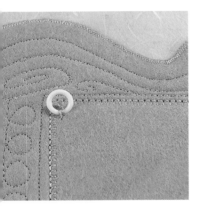

Curtain rings come in a variety of sizes and are easy to hand stitch to the back of a wall hanging as a hanging device.

Pillows

Painted silk also makes lovely pillow tops. You can add a border as described on page 27 for wall hangings, or use the piece as is. Cotton velveteen works well as a backing fabric for pillows and pillow-type dolls and stuffed animals.

For simple pillow construction, trim the completed pillow top so that the corners are neat and square, and trim your backing fabric to the same size. Stitch the front and back together, leaving an opening for stuffing with Polyfil or a pillow form. Stuff the pillow and hand stitch the opening closed. Refer to "Sewing-Machine Maintenance" on pages 23–25 for additional sewing tips.

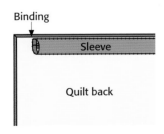

Binding

Sleeve

Quilt back

Fig. 11

If your pillow is elaborate or if you just want a pillow cover that you can remove easily, you can make a two-piece backing that closes with a zipper, buttons, or Velcro. To make this type of backing, cut two pieces of backing fabric so that they are oversized. Turn under one edge on each piece and install your zipper, work buttonholes, or stitch the Velcro in place. Close the pillow backing, and trim it to the same size as the pillow top. Then sew the front to the back as described above, only this time you don't need to leave an opening. You can put the pillow form in place through the opening (see fig. 12).

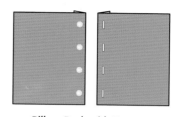

Pillow Back with Buttons

Fold under to create facing.
Work buttonholes in one half
of pillow back.
Sew buttons to other half.
Button the halves together and
trim back to fit the pillow front.

Fig. 12

Framing Your Art

Another fun way to showcase your painted silk project is to frame it behind glass. I recommend that you take your project to an experienced framer for this, since fabric needs to be treated with special care. Here are a few tips:

- ❀ Make sure that any backing material is acid free.
- ❀ Have the framer leave a space between the fabric and the glass of the frame, because fabric must be able to breath.
- ❀ Make sure moisture cannot get beneath the glass, where it can damage the fabric.
- ❀ Never hang your fabric art in direct sunlight.

Creating a Floor Cloth

MAKING A floor cloth is essentially creating a floor covering similar to vinyl or linoleum. Because the finished product will be just as stiff as linoleum, it should only be used on floors; placing a floor cloth on top of a carpet or a thick carpet pad will eventually cause the surface to crack. "Meow Box," the mailbox cover on page 87, and "Nice Kitty," the flowerpot and birdbath on page 93, were prepared and painted in the same way as the floor cloth "Watch Your Step!" on page 80, with two exceptions. They were both primed with Deka Sign Enamel primer instead of gesso because they will be used outdoors, and they did not require any clear finish to complete. Clear finishes or varnish tend to become foggy in appearance outdoors.

MATERIALS
Canvas

Most floor cloths are made of painted canvas. Preprimed floor cloth canvas is widely available at art supply stores or through mail-order catalogs. (See "Resources" on page 110 for ordering information.) It is primed on both sides and can be purchased by the foot off a roll or in a variety of precut sizes.

From top to bottom: Raw Artist's Canvas (10 ounces), Fredrix's Pre-primed Floor Cloth Canvas, and Kunin's Kreative Kanvas.

Deka Sign Enamel is a water-based, multi-use paint for indoor and outdoor use.

A new product from Kunin Felt called Kreative Kanvas is also suitable for floor cloths. It, too, is also available in precut sizes as well as by the foot, although it isn't preprimed. The floor cloth on page 80 is made of Kreative Kanvas, which I primed with one coat of gesso on each side. Most types of gesso are simply water-based primers that are used for coating canvas and wood. Gesso is available in both white and black.

Many artists purchase raw (unprimed) canvas for floor cloths. It must be primed on each side before cutting out the shape of the floor cloth because the canvas will shrink after priming. In fact, I recommend two coats of primer per side when working with raw canvas. Shrinking is not a problem with the preprimed floor cloth canvas or Kreative Kanvas.

To cut your canvas, you can use regular fabric shears, but you may not want to use your best scissors that you use for cutting other fabrics. Another alternative that works well is sharp craft scissors.

Paints

If you aren't using preprimed canvas, you'll need a can of gesso to prime your canvas. Once that's applied, you can use either oil or acrylic paints to paint the design, but I recommend Deka Sign Enamel paints, which are water-based acrylics. Enamel paints are very durable and give excellent coverage. They are very opaque so the colors layer well. When painting is complete, you'll need to cover the finished floor cloth with a protective coating that is suitable for the type of paint you used. I used three coats of Deka Sign Enamel Clear Coat finish to protect the floor cloth after painting with acrylics.

Brushes

I use a variety of shapes and sizes of paint brushes made specifically for use with acrylic paint for floor cloths. I also use some of the larger foam or rubber stamps, assorted sponges, and painting tools. You'll be ready for anything if you have a few flat brushes ranging in size from ¼" to 1"; round brushes in sizes 10, 6, and 2; and a 00 liner brush. I recommend rinsing your brushes often while painting to avoid paint build up.

Other Supplies

It's best to cover your work surface when working on a floor cloth. A drop cloth with a slick or shiny surface will be less likely to stick to the back of the canvas. I use a piece of vinyl and change the position of the floor cloth often to prevent sticking.

White butcher paper works well as pattern paper for floor cloths. Combined with graphite paper, which is available at craft stores, it will help you transfer your pattern to the canvas.

PREPARATION

Priming the Canvas

The first thing you need to do to your canvas is to prime it if you didn't purchase the preprimed variety. Brush on two coats of gesso to each side of the canvas, allowing it to dry completely between coats. If you are priming raw canvas, be sure to do it before you cut the canvas to size because it will shrink as the primer dries.

Hemming

I don't hem my floor cloths because I prefer nice flat edges. I do two things to help ensure that the floor cloth will lie flat. First, I make sure that the edges are well covered with each coat of gesso, paint, and Deka Sign Enamel Clear Coat. Second, I round off the corners rather than leave squared corners or edges. You can see this on the floor cloth on page 80.

If you prefer to hem a floor cloth, you'll need to allow for some extra canvas to turn under for the hem. Cut your canvas 4" longer and wider than specified in the project instructions so that you'll have 2" to turn under for a hem on each side of the floor cloth. To make a hem, use a long ruler or T-square to mark the 2" hem on all edges on the wrong side of the canvas. Fold the hem back along the marked lines; folding them over the ruler will help create a sharp crease. For a nice, neat hem, miter the corners. To do that, cut off a triangle of canvas at each corner, as shown in figure 13. Finally, glue the hems in place with glue suitable for fabrics, such as Sobo. You may have to place a weight on the hem so that it stays in place while the glue dries.

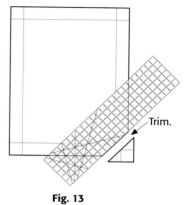

Trim.

Fig. 13

Transferring the Design

Enlarge the pattern on a photocopy machine according to the directions in the project. Place the pattern in position over the canvas and tape it in place with masking tape. Slide a sheet of graphite paper face down between the pattern and canvas, and draw over the design with a pencil. You may need to move the graphite paper from area to area. If you don't have graphite paper, you can make your own by rubbing a soft pencil across the back of the pattern where the lines are. Place the pattern over the canvas and tape it into position. Draw over the lines and the design will transfer to the canvas.

PAINTING

When painting a floor cloth, as with any painting project, think in terms of painting from the background to the foreground. Following manufacturer's directions, stir the paint well before using it. Use full-strength, or undiluted paint, for the overall design. Later, when adding more delicate lines and details, you can dilute the paint with a small amount of water so that the paint will flow more easily with your smaller liner brushes.

Painting tools include sponges, stamps, and a variety of other tools, including the Paint Eraser Tool (center bottom) and the Deer Foot Stippler brush from Loew-Cornell (center top), which is great for adding texture to backgrounds.

You can also create layers of glazes of varying degrees of transparency with diluted paint. The glazes may be lighter or darker in tone, depending on the effect you want. Glazes are great ways to shade or highlight. Once again, 35 millimeter film canisters make great containers for storing small amounts of mixed colors or diluted paint.

Besides painting with brushes, experiment with different types of sponges or some of the larger foam or rubber stamps. When using a sponge, dip it into the paint and dab it onto a paper towel to remove the excess paint before applying it to your floor cloth. Apply the paint to stamps with a foam brush. Paints may also be applied with stenciling techniques. There are also many painting tools on the market today that you can use to make fun and whimsical designs. Achieve different effects with the Paint Eraser Tool from Loew-Cornell or some of the home decorating tools like combs and paint dabbers.

Thicker glazes—more paint, less water—can be manipulated by removing some of the glaze with a paint eraser, comb, or sponges. You'll have to do this quickly, however, since acrylics dry fast. I usually apply the glaze in sections—approximately 4" by 4". Wait for a few seconds; then use one of the tools to remove some of the paint or move it around to create textures or variations. Experiment and have fun!

FINISHING TOUCHES

After painting most of the larger areas of color on your cloth, you may need to realign the pattern over the canvas and transfer details for things such as a face or a flower shape. If the paint is too dark for graphite lines to show, rub chalk or chalk pencil on the back of the pattern in a lighter color. You can then transfer the chalk lines to the surface by drawing over the lines with a pencil. You can also buy light-colored transfer papers, such as Saral brand (available in fabric shops), if you don't want to make your own.

After completing all the painting, allow your floor cloth to dry thoroughly. Acrylic paints will quickly appear dry to the touch—in about fifteen minutes. However, you should wait two to four hours before handling the floor cloth and four to eight hours before recoating it. Once the paint is dry, turn the floor cloth over. Paint a 1" border of the same color as the background on the back of the floor cloth to help make the edges a bit more durable and to give a nice finishing touch to the whole project. Allow the paint to dry thoroughly. Then, following manufacturer's directions, apply a protective coating such as Deka Sign Enamel Clear Coat finish to the surface. With Deka Sign Enamel Clear Coat, three coats are recommended, and you must let each one dry before adding the next coat. For best results, allow the paint to cure for one week before using the floor cloth.

To complete the floor cloth, cut a piece of no-skid rug mat 1" smaller than the floor cloth on all sides. Place the mat in position and put the floor cloth on top. To maintain the floor cloth, wipe it clean periodically with a damp cloth.

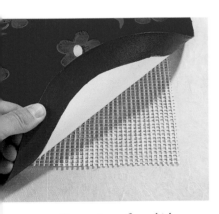

Cut a piece of no-skid mat to use underneath a floor cloth to prevent slipping.

Mild detergent may be used for heavier spills. Avoid creasing it, because this will eventually lead to cracks in the surface. With proper care, floor cloths will last for years.

Painting Wood

PAINTED WOOD decorations are so popular today. But why buy the same thing that everyone else has when you can easily create your own custom designs? You can set your garden apart from the crowd with "Cat Crossing," which is the painted garden sign on page 98, or adapt one of the other designs to paint on wood.

MATERIALS

When painting wood for outside use, it's important to use a marine plywood or pressure-treated wood that can stand up to all sorts of weather. For "Cat Crossing," I purchased treated wood at a home improvement store, where they cut it to my desired size.

You can use the same paints as those used for the floor cloth, the mailbox cover, and the cat flowerpot and birdbath—Deka Sign Enamel paints. They are water-based, formulated for indoor and outdoor use, very durable, and lightfast. You'll also need to apply Deka Sign Enamel primer before painting.

Other supplies to have on hand include medium- and fine-grade sandpaper, paper large enough to trace the pattern, graphite paper, a pencil, and an assortment of paint brushes.

PREPARATION

To prepare the wood, sand the surface and edges, starting with the medium-grade sandpaper. Finish by lightly sanding with the fine-grade sandpaper. Brush off the dust after sanding, and wipe the wood with a clean, dry, lint-free cloth to remove any remaining dust. Apply an even coat of primer. If you wish, you can lightly sand the wood with the fine-grade sandpaper after the primer is dry.

Enlarge the pattern on a photocopy machine according to the directions in the project. Tape the pattern sections together or trace the sections onto one large sheet of white paper. Position the pattern over the wood and transfer the design to the wood with purchased graphite paper. Or, if you prefer, you can make your own transfer paper by rubbing a soft pencil or chalk on the back of the pattern. When the pattern is in place on the wood, trace over the pattern lines with a pencil to transfer the design.

PAINTING THE DESIGN

Always read the manufacturer's instructions before using any product. I also recommend practicing on scrap material before working on the actual project. Stir the paint well before using. Always think in terms of painting from the background to the foreground. Use full-strength, or undiluted paint, for the overall design. Later, when adding more delicate lines and fine details, you can dilute the paint with a small amount of water to help the paint flow more easily when you're using smaller liner brushes.

You can also create layers of glazes of varying degrees of transparency with the diluted paint. The glazes may be lighter or darker in tone, depending on the effect you want. Glazes are great ways to shade or highlight.

After painting most of the larger areas of color, you may need to realign the pattern over the surface and transfer smaller details. If the paint is too dark for the graphite lines to show, rub chalk or a chalk pencil on the back of the pattern in a lighter color. You can then transfer the chalk lines to the surface by drawing over the lines with a pencil.

Besides painting with brushes, experiment with different types of sponges or some of the larger foam or rubber stamps. When using a sponge, dab it into the paint and then onto a paper towel to remove excess paint before painting with it. Apply paint to stamps with a foam brush. The paints may also be applied with stenciling techniques. See "Painting the Design" under "Painting Glass and Glazed Ceramics" on page 36 for more ideas and tools to create special effects.

FINISHING

When using Deka Sign Enamel paints for outdoor projects, there is no need to apply a clear finish. The enamel paint is durable and designed for outdoor use. In fact, clear finishes tend to become foggy on items that are placed outdoors.

Painting Glass and Glazed Ceramics

PAINTING GLASSWARE and ceramics is a great way to create custom projects for your home and to make unique gifts. You can find many inexpensive pieces at home and at discount stores. I always paint several things for gifts each year. The painted glass and ceramic projects in this book include "Platter Puss" on page 103, which is a glass platter, and "Mouse and Cookies," a ceramic mug and plate on page 106.

MATERIALS

For the glass platter, I used Pébéo's Vitrea 160 outline paint and paints for glass. For the ceramic mug and plate, I used Pébéo's Porcelaine 150 paints. Both paints are water based and are also available as markers. Pébéo's Porcelaine 150 paints resemble enamel after baking and are not transparent like Pébéo's

Vitrea paints. You may apply the paints directly, or you may prefer to create the look of stained glass by outlining each section before applying any paint. Outline paint resembles the leading in stained glass and is available in both Pébéo's Vitrea 160 and Porcelaine 150 paints. Once the design is outlined, each area of color is painted within the drawn lines. To apply the paint, use soft brushes in an assortment of rounds and flats in small sizes. You can also use sponges to apply the paints. Finally, both kinds of paint need to be heat-set in the oven to make them durable. With proper care, your glass and ceramic projects will last indefinitely.

Pébéo paints do not contain lead and are made of nontoxic materials. Inadvertent contact of the completed projects with food or drink is not a health hazard. However, these paints are *not* approved for items that will store food or drink.

If you are working with glassware, you can either put your pattern underneath or inside the glass and use it as a guide for painting. Or, you can use a china marker to draw the design on the surface before painting. China markers look like pencils, but they are waxy and easily rub off glass surfaces. For ceramics, you'll need graphite paper or Pébéo's transfer paper so that you can trace over the pattern and transfer the design onto the clay surface.

Pébéo's Vitrea 160 glass paints and Porcelaine 150 ceramic paints also come in outline paints and markers to make outlining and highlighting easy.

PREPARATION

The most important step in preparing glass or ceramic for painting is to wash it with warm, soapy water. Dry each piece with a clean towel and set it aside. If there is any dirt or oil on the surface, the paint won't adhere properly.

For glassware, prepare the pattern and make sure it fits your particular piece. If necessary, enlarge the pattern on a photocopy machine according to the directions in the project. Then tape the pattern into position. For plates or bowls, tape the pattern to the top surface of the dish. Turn the glassware over and follow the pattern to apply the paint to the bottom or outside surface of the glass. For vases or glasses, tape the pattern to the inside of the piece. Stuff crumpled paper towels or tissue paper inside the piece to help hold the pattern flat against the inner surface.

For ceramics, graphite paper may be used to transfer designs to the surface, but it's best to do this sparingly. Too heavy of a build-up of graphite lines can prevent paint from adhering. Tape the pattern into position with the graphite paper face down between the pattern and the surface of the object. Trace the design with a fine-point pencil.

I always recommend practicing first before beginning a project. As long as the paints aren't heat set, they can be removed with water or rubbing alcohol. Practice on the actual piece or on a separate piece of glass or ceramic. I use a variety of soft brushes—flats and rounds—in different sizes. Flat brushes are great for painting checkerboard designs and stripes; use the width of the brush to determine the width and spacing. That's how I made the red checkerboard on the mug and plate for "Mouse and Cookies" on page 106.

I used a ½"-wide flat brush to paint the checkerboard design on this plate. The brush makes a great guide for judging your spacing.

PAINTING THE DESIGN

If you plan to use outline paint, apply it first. Then you can fill in the areas of color with a brush or a sponge. The angle at which you hold the brush will affect how the paint flows onto your glass or ceramic ware. The amount of pressure you use is also factor. I often hold my brush almost flat against the surface as I work, exerting very little pressure, because I find I get better paint coverage. This technique is hard to do with a stiff brush, so you'll definitely want to follow my recommendation and use soft brushes!

Sponges also work well for painting glass and ceramics. I've used everything from natural sea sponges to make-up wedges. Each type of sponge will create a different texture. And you can easily cut them into smaller pieces to accommodate a particular need. Sponges clean up easily with soap and water.

You can create lovely color variations by layering colors and even mixing colors on the surface of the glass or ceramic. You can also create new colors by mixing the paints before using them. For lighter tints, mix color paints with white or a dilutant such as Pébéo water-based dilutant.

HEAT SETTING

Allow at least twenty-four hours of drying time before heat setting the paint on glassware or ceramic pieces. For the Vitrea paints, place the glassware in a cool oven and set the oven for 325° F. After the oven temperature reaches 325° F, set the timer for forty minutes. When the timer beeps, turn the oven off, open the door, and allow the glass to cool gradually in the oven before removing it.

For the ceramics painted with the Porcelaine 150 paint, place them in a cool oven and set the temperature for 300° F. After the oven has reached that temperature, set the timer for thirty-five minutes. When baking is complete, turn the oven off, open the door, and allow the ceramic pieces to cool gradually in the oven.

Both types of paint are lightfast and durable, so they will hold up well when washing your painted pieces. While the manufacturer and some artists I know say they've washed painted pieces in the dishwasher, I haven't tried it myself. After putting time and effort into creating a one-of-a-kind piece, I prefer to simply hand wash my glass and ceramic items.

Projects

FISHFUL THINKING
Painted Silk Scarf

Materials

- ❀ Prehemmed white silk scarf, 11" x 40"
- ❀ Soap for hand washables, or mild shampoo
- ❀ Pattern
- ❀ Soft lead pencil
- ❀ Wooden stretcher bars:
    - 2 strips, each 44"
    - 2 strips, each 14"
- ❀ Deka Silk tacks
- ❀ Deka black and clear resist
- ❀ Deka metal applicator tip
- ❀ Deka Silk paints in buttercup yellow, ebony, mint green, cinnamon, tangerine, rose, deep lilac, and royal blue
- ❀ Containers for water and for mixing or diluting paints
- ❀ 2 or 3 sizes of round watercolor brushes and a 1"-wide foam brush

Pattern Enlarging

THE GRAY-AND-WHITE tabby cat pattern on page 40 and the brown tabby cat pattern on page 41 will need to be enlarged 150 percent. The fish patterns on pages 41 and 42 do not need to be enlarged.

Preparation

READ "Silk Painting Basics" on pages 13–19 before beginning the project.

FISHFUL THINKING *by Sheila Haynes Rauen, 1999, Knoxville, Tennessee, 11" x 40". This design combines two cats with another wonderful subject for silk painting—fish. Tropical fish are so lovely and colorful that you can have fun experimenting with different colors and combinations when painting them.*

1. Prepare the silk and stretch it onto the frame. Prepare the pattern and transfer the design to the silk.

2. Apply the black resist to outline the faces of the cats and the black dots for the eyes of the fish. Be sure to use the metal tip on the end of the resist bottle for better control.

3. After the black resist has dried for a few minutes, apply the clear resist to create the rest of the design, using the photograph on page 38 as a guide. Allow all resist to dry for 1 hour before painting.

   NOTE: *The white areas on the gray cat were outlined with clear resist and then left unpainted so they would remain white on the scarf. It's unnecessary to fill in large areas you wish to remain white with large amounts of resist. Simply outline them and leave them unpainted.*

Gray-and-white cat

Painting

1. Paint the eyes of the gray-and-white cat buttercup yellow.

2. Paint the gray-and-white cat's head and body with a mixture of ebony paint and water. You may want to start with a half-and-half mixture and add more water or paint depending on whether you want a lighter or darker gray.

3. With just a touch of diluted gray paint and a small brush, add shading under the cat's eyes and on his muzzle.

4. Paint the brown tabby cat's eyes mint green.

5. On the brown tabby cat, paint the dark markings and nose cinnamon.

6. Paint the brown tabby cat's head and body a light brown with a mixture of the cinnamon paint and water.

7. For the fish, don't be afraid to experiment with different colors. My green fish and the orange fish were first painted buttercup yellow. I added small amounts of tangerine, rose, and mint green to the wet yellow paint to create color variations. The violet fish started out as deep lilac with buttercup yellow markings. I added tangerine to both colors to create shading and additional colors.

8. Mix royal blue with water to create your background color. Begin with 1 to 2 ounces of water, and add small amounts of paint until you reach the desired tint of blue. Paint the entire background with a 1"-wide foam brush or large watercolor-wash brush. Overlap your strokes as you paint.

9. Cure, heat-set, and press the silk as described in "Heat Setting and Care of Painted Silk" on page 18.

Brown tabby cat

Tropical fish

Gray-and-White Cat
Enlarge pattern 150 percent.

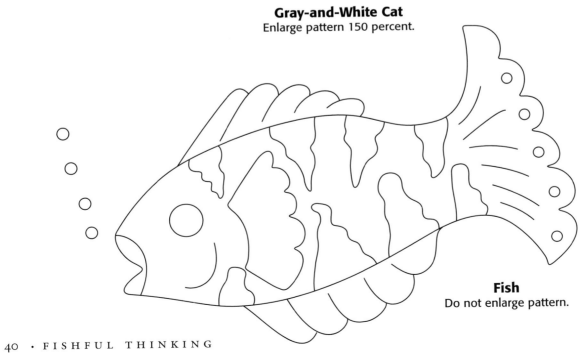

Fish
Do not enlarge pattern.

Brown Tabby Cat
Enlarge pattern 150 percent.

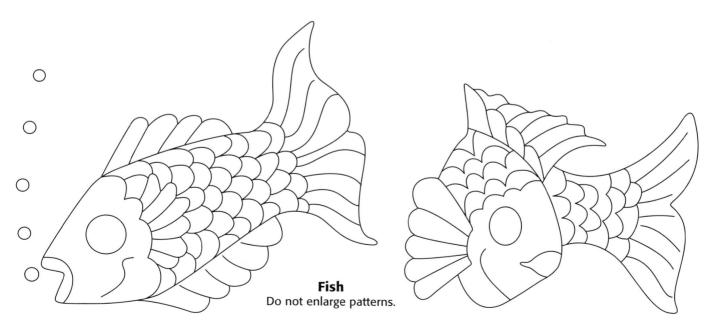

Fish
Do not enlarge patterns.

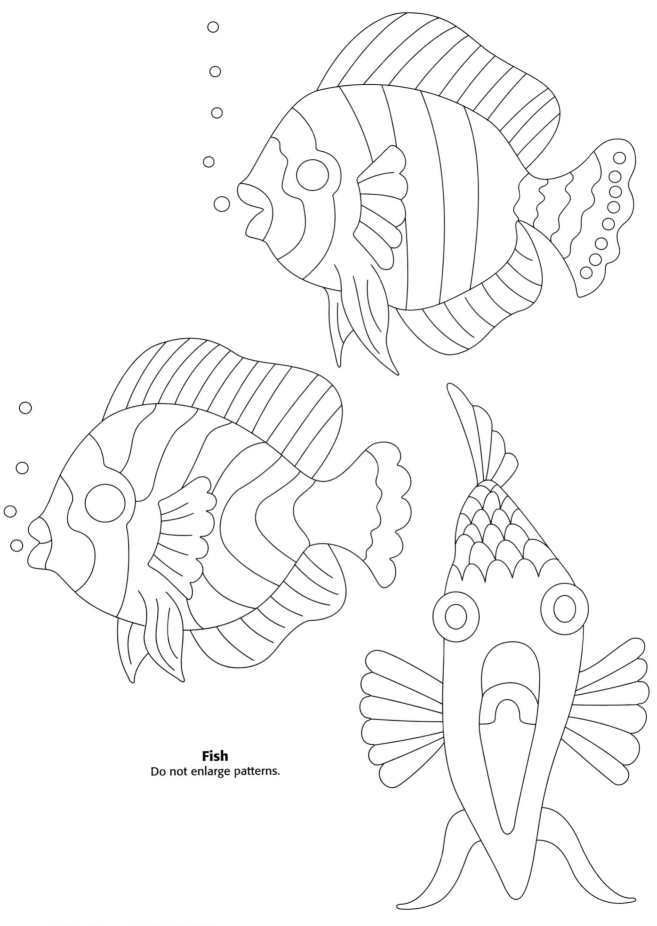

Fish
Do not enlarge patterns.

KITTY KUSHION *Painted and Quilted Silk Pillow*

KITTY KUSHION *by Sheila Haynes Rauen, 1999, Knoxville, Tennessee, 15½" x 15½". I used warm orange and cinnamon brown for my Kitty Kushion. You can follow my color scheme, or make up your own to honor your favorite feline friend.*

*Don't make just one of these!
Flip the pattern over to create
a mirror image so you can
have two kitties snuggling up
together on your coziest chair
or sofa.*

Materials

- ❀ 20" x 20" square of white silk (China silk or crepe de chine in 8mm or 10mm thickness)
- ❀ Soap for hand washables, or mild shampoo
- ❀ Stretcher bars for frame: 4 bars, each 20"
- ❀ Deka Silk tacks
- ❀ Enlarged pattern
- ❀ Soft lead pencil
- ❀ Deka Silk black and clear resist
- ❀ Deka Silk metal applicator tip
- ❀ Deka Silk paints in mint green, ebony, cinnamon, buttercup yellow, tangerine, and chestnut
- ❀ Containers for water and for mixing or diluting paints
- ❀ Assorted sizes of watercolor brushes
- ❀ 20" square of muslin
- ❀ 20" square of low-loft cotton batting
- ❀ 20" square of black velveteen for pillow back
- ❀ Safety pins or basting spray
- ❀ Machine quilting thread
- ❀ Sewing thread
- ❀ Stuffing
- ❀ 16" square pillow form

Pattern Enlarging

THE CAT pattern on page 46 will need to be enlarged 250 percent. Since some photocopiers only enlarge to 150 percent, you may need to enlarge the pattern in three steps. First, enlarge the pattern 150 percent. Take the photocopy of the pattern and place it onto the photocopy machine; enlarge it by 150 percent. Place this photocopy on the copier and enlarge it 111 percent. You will have to enlarge the pattern in sections and tape the pieces together.

Painting

BE SURE to read "Silk Painting Basics" on page 13–19 and "Pillows" on pages 28–29 before beginning the project.

1. Prepare the silk and stretch it onto the frame. Prepare the pattern and transfer the design to the silk.

2. Using the photograph on page 43 as a guide, apply black resist to outline the cat's eyes, nose, and mouth.

3. After the black resist has dried for a few minutes, apply clear resist to outline the fur color variations, legs, paws, tail, ears, highlights in the eyes and on the nose, and the remaining lines on the face of the cat. Allow all resist to dry for 1 hour before painting.

4. Paint the cat's eyes mint green and the pupils ebony.

5. Paint the dark fur patches on the cat cinnamon.

6. Mix 2 tints—one of cinnamon and water, and one of buttercup yellow and water—to use for the lighter areas on the cat's body. You may add a small amount of tangerine for more of an orange color. Finish painting the cat with the lighter tints.

7. With water and cinnamon paint, mix a small amount of a very light tint of cinnamon for the light areas above and below the cat's eyes. Allow all paint to dry before adding details.

8. When the paint is dry, use a small round brush with a very small amount of diluted cinnamon paint to add dark lines around the eyes, nose, mouth, head, and back leg of the cat.

9. Dilute a small amount of chestnut paint and with a small brush, paint additional squiggles to create more texture on the cat's head and body.

10. Following the directions on page 18, heat-set the paint. Do not trim the edges of the silk yet.

Quilting and Pillow Construction

1. Cut a 20" square each from the muslin, batting, and velveteen. Set the velveteen aside.

2. Layer the muslin with the batting, followed by the painted silk on top so that the design is facing upward. Baste the 3 layers together with safety pins or a combination of basting spray and pins.

3. Using black thread for the outline of the cat's eyes, nose, and mouth, and white thread for the rest of the design, quilt along the resist lines with a straight stitch. Work from the center of the design, radiating outward.

4. Add extra whiskers to the cat by hand. Thread a needle with double thread. From the outside, push the needle in and back out, tying a double or triple knot and cutting the threads so that the whiskers are approximately 2" long.

5. With the design facing upward, stitch all around the outer edge of the cat, through all 3 layers. This line of stitching will be your guide as you stitch the velveteen backing fabric to the pillow, so stitch carefully. The final size of the pillow should be approximately 15½" square, plus the ears, to accommodate the 16" pillow form. I find that it's usually best to make a pillow covering slightly smaller than the pillow form for a nice, plump pillow.

I used black thread to quilt around the eyes, nose, and mouth.

6. With right sides together, sew the velveteen to the painted and quilted front of the pillow by using the stitching guideline you created in step 5. Leave an opening at the bottom of the pillow so that you can insert the pillow form. Reinforce the stitching at all corners, including the ears.

7. Trim the excess fabric, leaving about a ½" seam allowance. Clip the corners at the cat's ears and turn the pillow cover right side out.

8. Stuff the cat's ears with stuffing before inserting the pillow form or other stuffing. When the pillow form is in place, stitch the opening closed by hand with a simple whipstitch.

Cat
Enlarge pattern 250 percent.

ANGEL GABRIEL
Painted Silk Cat with Quilted Silk Wings

ANGEL GABRIEL by Sheila Haynes Rauen, 2000, Knoxville, Tennessee, 7" x 9". My Persian cat boss is named Gabriel. I always refer to him as my angel Gabriel (even though I named him after the British singer Peter Gabriel). I thought that it's only fitting that I include a cat angel in the projects! If your kitten is more of a little devil, skip the wings and make a nice set of horns instead.

Materials

- ⅓ yd. of 8mm or 10mm white silk
- Soap for hand washables, or mild shampoo
- Stretcher bars for frame:
    - 2 bars, each 10"
    - 2 bars, each 12"
- Pattern
- Deka Silk tacks
- Soft lead pencil
- Deka Silk black and clear resists
- Deka Silk metal applicator tip
- Deka Silk paints in buttercup yellow and ebony
- Small- and medium-size round watercolor brushes
- Containers for mixing paint and for water
- 9" x 12" piece of muslin
- 9" x 12" piece of black velveteen
- Basting spray
- Sewing thread
- Bobbin thread
- Quilting thread
- Stuffing
- 8" x 4" piece of batting
- Gold thread or cording (optional)

Painting

BE SURE to read "Silk Painting Basics" on pages 13–19 and "Pillows" on pages 28–29 before beginning the project. The project patterns are on pages 50–51 and do not need to be enlarged.

1. Prepare a 9" x 12" piece of silk and stretch it onto the frame. Prepare the pattern and transfer the design to the silk.

2. Using the photograph on page 47 as a guide, apply black resist to eyes, nose, mouth, whiskers, legs, paws, and tail.

3. After the black resist has dried for a few minutes, apply clear resist to outline the white areas on the face, chest, paws, eye highlights, and white lines in the fur. Allow all resist to dry for 1 hour.

4. Paint the eyes with buttercup yellow and a small, round watercolor brush.

5. Using one part ebony to one part water, mix a small amount of gray paint for the cat. Paint the head and body of the cat with the gray mixture.

6. Cure, heat-set, and press the silk as described in "Heat Setting and Care of Painted Silk" on page 18.

7. Cut out the cat, leaving a ½" seam allowance all around.

8. Lay the cat on top of the muslin and velveteen to use as a pattern for cutting out these fabrics. Be sure that the velveteen is facing right side down while the cat is facing right side up so that your finished pillow backing will face the correct direction outward when the cat angel is complete.

9. Spray-baste the muslin to the wrong side of the painted silk to stabilize the fabric before constructing the cat. Stitch around the cat along the desired stitching line. You won't want to cut off any design elements or leave unpainted areas showing. This line will serve as a stitching guide when you assemble the cat angel.

10. Pin the front and back pieces of the cat together with right sides together. Stitch around from the bottom, leaving an opening for turning. Reinforce the stitching at the corners. Clip the corners at the ears so that they will turn right side out without puckering.

11. Turn the cat right side out and stuff firmly with stuffing. Hand stitch the opening closed.

12. Trace the wing design onto your remaining silk and 8" x 4" piece of batting. Cut 2 silk wing pieces and 1 wing piece from the thin batting.

13. Layer the wing pieces so that the batting is on the bottom, followed by the 2 silk pieces with right sides together. (The wing design should be traced on the right side of the silk pieces.) Pin the pieces together. Stitch around the wings, leaving an opening for turning. Trim the seams and turn the wings right side out. The batting will now be on the inside, between the layers of silk.

14. Using the drawn lines on the wings as a guide, machine stitch the details on the wings.

Sew quilted wings in place by hand with quilting thread.

15. Using quilting thread, attach the wings to the cat by hand so that the stitches are hidden underneath the wings. Stitch the center of the wings to the cat, leaving the ends of the wings free.

16. If you want to hang your angel cat, sew a loop of gold thread or cording to the back. This thread could double as a halo if you sew it to the back of the angel cat's head.

Cat
Do not enlarge pattern.

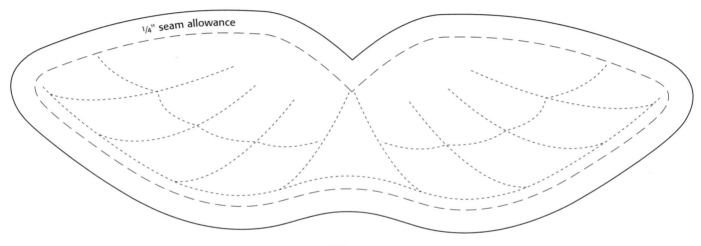

¼" seam allowance

Wings
Do not enlarge pattern.

TUBE 'N TABBY

Painted Silk Picture with Painted Wooden Frame

Tꜱᴜʙᴇ 'ɴ Tᴀʙʙʏ *by Sheila Haynes Rauen, 2000, Knoxville, Tennessee, 16½" x 21". I have to admit that this painting is really a self-portrait. One of my favorite pastimes at the lake is to float around in my little inflatable boat. (I'm not quite as trusting as Tabby regarding what might be swimming around or under me!) I was contemplating life one day while floating, thinking it doesn't get much better than this, when the image of "Tube 'n Tabby" came to me. Will all of the poor fish meet with the same fate? I'll never tell!*

The frame around Tabby was purchased unfinished and stained with ebony silk paint, which makes a nice wood stain, as you can see. The fish were painted with acrylic enamel paint that I use for floor cloths.

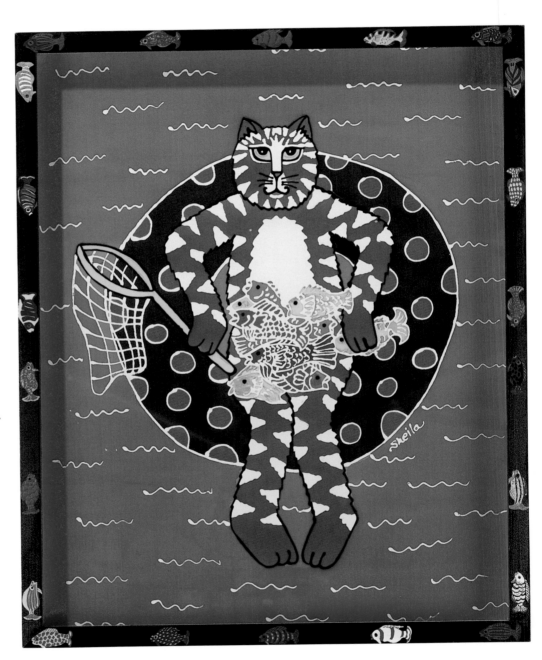

Materials

- ⅔ yd. of 8mm or 10mm white silk
- Soap for hand washables, or mild shampoo
- Stretcher bars for frame:
    - 2 bars, each 20"
    - 2 bars, each 24"
- Deka Silk tacks
- Pattern
- Soft lead pencil
- Deka Silk black and clear resist
- Deka Silk metal applicator tip
- Deka Silk paints in ebony, cherry, cinnamon, buttercup yellow, skyline blue, turquoise, mint green, deep lilac, and rose
- 2 or 3 sizes of round watercolor brushes and a 1"-wide foam brush for silk paints
- Containers for water and for mixing or diluting paints
- Unfinished wood frame, 18" x 22½"
- Sandpaper
- Chalk or light-colored transfer paper
- Acrylic paints in desired colors for fish on frame
- Small brushes for acrylic paints
- Water-based, clear protective finish
- Acid-free foam or mat board

Enlarging the Pattern

THE CAT pattern on page 55 will need to be enlarged 200 percent. Since some photocopiers only enlarge to 150 percent, you may need to enlarge the pattern in two steps. First, enlarge the pattern 150 percent. Then take the photocopy of the pattern and place it onto the photocopy machine; enlarge it by 133 percent. You will have to do the pattern in sections and tape the pieces together. Please note that the fish pattern for the frame does not need to be enlarged.

Painting the Silk

BE SURE to read "Silk Painting Basics" on pages 13–19 and "Framing Your Art" on page 29 before beginning the project.

1. Prepare a 20" x 24" piece of silk and stretch it onto the frame. Prepare the pattern and transfer the design to the silk.

Use clear resist to outline the cat's white areas and eye highlights.

Outline the fish with clear resist. Use black resist for the eyes.

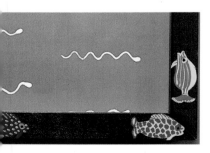

Paint fish with acrylic enamel paint.

2. Using the photograph on page 52 as a guide, apply black resist to the cat's face and to outline its body. Outline the handle and frame for the fish net, and draw a dot for each fish eye. Allow the black resist to dry for a few minutes before applying clear resist.

3. After the black resist has dried, apply clear resist to outline the white areas on the cat and the highlights in the cat's eyes.

4. Outline the fish, the net, the inner tube, and the wavy lines in the water with clear resist. Allow all resist to dry for 1 hour before painting.

5. Paint the inner tube ebony with cherry polka dots.

6. Paint the cat's face and body cinnamon.

7. Paint the handle and frame for the fish net, the cat's eyes, and some of the fish buttercup yellow.

8. Paint the water skyline blue with the 1"-wide foam brush. Make overlapping strokes when filling in large areas of color.

9. Paint the remaining fish turquoise, mint green, deep lilac, and rose.

10. After the yellow in the cat's eyes dries, use a very small brush with a very small amount of mint green paint to take a curving stroke under the pupil of the eye.

11. Cure, heat-set, and press the silk as described in "Heat Setting and Care of Painted Silk" on page 18. Do not cut around the design. The extra fabric will be needed to overlap the mounting board when framing.

Painting the Frame

READ "Painting Wood" on pages 33–34 before beginning this part of the project.

1. Sand the unfinished wood frame and brush off the dust.

2. Using the 1"-wide foam brush, stain the wood with the ebony silk paint. Wipe off the excess stain with a clean, dry cloth such as an old tee shirt. Allow the paint to dry thoroughly before painting the fish on the frame.

3. With light-colored transfer paper or by making your own transfer paper with chalk, transfer the fish pattern on page 55 to the frame.

4. Paint fish in a variety of colors with different markings. Use acrylic enamel paints or other acrylic paints.

5. When the fish are dry, apply 1 to 3 coats of protective finish to the frame.

6. When framing your fabric, it is very important to mount it onto acid-free foam board or mat board. Also, leave some space between the fabric and the glass so that the fabric, which is a natural fiber, can breathe. For more on framing, see page 29.

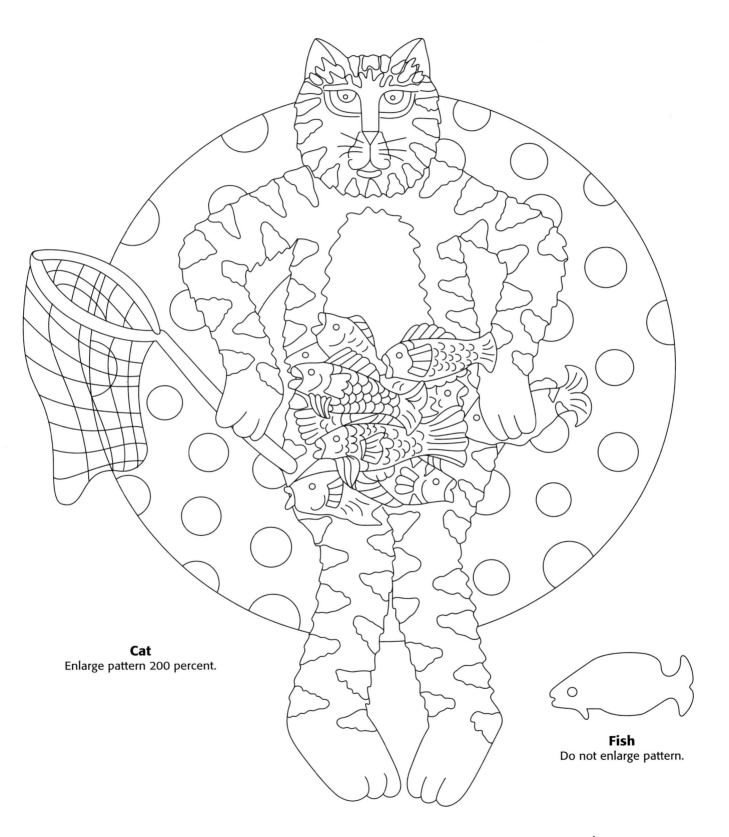

Cat
Enlarge pattern 200 percent.

Fish
Do not enlarge pattern.

A ROOM WITH A MOUSE *Painted Silk Wall Hanging*

A ROOM WITH A MOUSE *by Sheila Haynes Rauen, 1999, Knoxville, Tennessee, 16½" x 21". Are they friends or is this a temporary truce? They look pretty comfortable to me. This design was inspired by the way my cats drape themselves on the furniture. It's a good example of how to create patterns and textures with free-motion embroidery. The image is first painted on silk with the Deka Silk stop-flow primer method. Then machine embroidery is stitched through three layers to create a quilted picture. I also quilted the velveteen frame with gold metallic thread.*

Materials

- ❀ ½ yd. 8mm or 10mm silk
- ❀ Soap for hand-washables, or mild shampoo
- ❀ Stretcher bars for frame:
    2 bars, each 14"
    2 bars, each 18"
- ❀ Deka Silk tacks
- ❀ Pattern
- ❀ Deka Silk stop-flow primer
- ❀ 1"-wide foam brush
- ❀ Soft lead pencil
- ❀ Deka Silk paints in buttercup yellow, royal blue, cherry, mint green, cinnamon, and ebony
- ❀ Deka permanent fabric paint in metallic gold
- ❀ 2 or 3 sizes of round watercolor brushes and 1 small round for details
- ❀ Containers for water and for mixing and diluting paints
- ❀ ½ yd. low-loft quilt batting
- ❀ ½ yd. muslin
- ❀ Basting spray or safety pins
- ❀ Darning foot
- ❀ Thread in white, medium green, red, blue, yellow, gray, black, brown, light orange, and metallic gold for machine embroidery
- ❀ Embroidery, universal, and metalfil needles
- ❀ Bobbin thread
- ❀ Embroidery hoop
- ❀ Sewing thread
- ❀ ½ yd. black cotton velveteen

Enlarging the Pattern

THE PATTERN on page 60 will need to be enlarged 200 percent. Since some photocopiers only enlarge to 150 percent, you may need to enlarge the pattern in two steps. First, enlarge the pattern 150 percent. Then take the photocopy of the pattern and place it onto the photocopy machine; enlarge it by 133 percent. You will have to enlarge the pattern in sections and tape the pieces together.

Painting the Silk

BE SURE to read "Silk Painting Basics" on pages 13–19 and "Embellishing with Free-Motion Embroidery and Quilting" on pages 23–29 before beginning the project.

1. Prepare a 14" x 18" piece of silk and stretch it onto the frame. Prepare the pattern.

2. Apply Deka Silk stop-flow primer evenly to the stretched silk with the 1"-wide foam brush. Allow the primer to dry thoroughly before applying a second coat, which is needed if you're using 10mm or thicker silk.

3. Trace the pattern lightly onto the dry silk with a pencil.

4. Paint the background, the sun in the picture, and the flower centers in the small picture buttercup yellow.

5. Paint the rug, the sky outside the window, and the sky in the small picture with diluted royal blue paint.

6. Paint the red stripes on the chair, the bird, the flowers in the small picture, and the curtain valance with cherry paint.

7. Paint the apple tree and cat's eyes mint green. (The apples are embroidered.)

8. Paint the woodwork, window trim, chair feet, and mouse cinnamon.

9. Paint the floor squares ebony.

10. Using a mixture of water and ebony paint, paint the cat gray.

11. Paint the small picture frame with metallic gold fabric paint.

12. Cure, heat-set, and press the silk as described in "Heat Setting and Care of Painted Silk" on page 18 before you make the quilt.

Free-Motion Embroidery and Quilting

1. Cut a piece of quilt batting and muslin the same size as the silk painting.

2. Baste the 3 layers together with muslin first, batting second, and the silk painting on top, right side facing up.

3. Use a darning foot on your sewing machine for free-motion embroidery (see page 23). Start with white embroidery thread in the top, and bobbin thread.

4. Referring to "To Hoop or Not to Hoop" on page 25, install the center of the design in your embroidery hoop and quilt the straight lines on the stripes of the chair. Be sure to lower the feed dogs.

Cat in chair

5. Using the photographs at right and on page 59 as a guide, continue free-motion embroidery in the appropriate colors, working from the center outward. You will need to change the top thread and move the hoop often. Refer to the photos for ideas on how you can use various thread colors and stitch patterns to embellish your quilt.

6. The wallpaper design is stitched—not painted—with medium green thread for the vine and leaves. Flower swirls along the vines were stitched with red thread. I stitched over the swirls 2 or 3 times to emphasize them.

Making the Wall Hanging

1. Remove any pins from the fabric and press the quilt lightly from the wrong side. Trim the quilted fabric to 12½" by 16", which allows for a ½" seam allow-ance when adding the border.

2. With the design facing up, stitch around the entire picture along the desired stitching line. You won't want to cut off any design elements or leave unpaint-ed areas showing. This will create a stitching line for adding the border, ensuring that you won't obscure any important design elements.

3. Cut 2 strips of velveteen, each 3¼" x 15¼", and 2 strips of batting the same size. Pin the velveteen strips to the sides of the quilted picture, right sides together. Layer the batting behind the velveteen. Stitch the velveteen and batting strips to the sides of the quilt along the stitching line. Trim the seams if desired and press the seams toward the border.

4. Cut 2 strips of velveteen and 2 strips of batting, each 3¼" x 17¼", for the top and bottom borders. Pin and stitch the velveteen and batting in place, as before. Trim the seams if desired, and iron the seams toward border.

5. Cut a 15¼" x 17¼" piece of muslin for the quilt backing. With right sides together, stitch the backing to the quilt top, leaving an opening for turning. Reinforce the stitching at the corners. Trim the seams and clip the corners diagonally.

6. Turn the quilt top right side out. Press the edges carefully so that the muslin backing doesn't show along the edges of the velveteen borders, and slipstitch the opening closed.

7. Using a metalfil needle, metallic gold embroidery thread, and bobbin thread, quilt the velveteen border to create the look of a frame. Because of the nap of the fabric, you may want to use longer than usual stitches so that the thread will show up and not get lost in the nap.

8. Referring to "Hanging Your Art" on page 28, add a hanging sleeve.

Window details

Wallpaper design

Quilt the velveteen border.

Wall Hanging
Enlarge pattern 200 percent.

BOWL ME OVER *Painted Silk Wall Hanging*

BOWL ME OVER *by Sheila Haynes Rauen, 1999, Knoxville, Tennessee, 14" x 15½". I originally made this fishbowl design as an interpretation of a mask for an artists' challenge at a local art gallery. While there are actually little eyeholes cut out of my cat's eyes, you can simply make this as an amusing little wall hanging, adding a few seed beads for extra dimension and whimsy. I find it very intriguing to see how things are distorted when viewed through curved glass and water. I'm sure our feline friend is more focused on the fish than anything else though!*

Materials

- ½ yd. 8mm or 10mm white silk
- Soap for hand washables, or mild shampoo
- Stretcher bars for frame
    - 2 bars, 18"
    - 2 bars, 20"
- Deka Silk tacks
- Pattern
- Deka Silk stop-flow primer
- 1"-wide foam brush
- Soft lead pencil
- Deka Silk paints in cherry, royal blue, buttercup yellow, chestnut brown, cinnamon, mint green, and ebony
- 2 or 3 sizes of round watercolor brushes
- Containers for water and for mixing and diluting paints
- ½ yd. muslin
- ½ yd. low-loft quilt batting
- Basting spray or long quilting pins
- Embroidery hoop
- Darning foot
- Bobbin thread
- Thread in light tan, black, red, yellow, light green, dark brown, medium brown, medium green, turquoise, white, and metallic silver for machine embroidery
- Clear seed beads (about 18) and beading needle
- ¼ yd. gold dupioni silk for border
- Sewing thread

Enlarging the Pattern

THE PATTERN on page 65 will need to be enlarged 200 percent. Since some photocopiers only enlarge to 150 percent, you need to enlarge the pattern in two steps. First, enlarge the pattern 150 percent. Then take the photocopy of the pattern and place it onto the photocopy machine; enlarge it by 133 percent. You will have to do the pattern in sections and tape the pieces together.

Painting the Silk

READ "Silk Painting Basics" on pages 13–19 and "Embellishing with Free-Motion Embroidery and Quilting" on pages 23–29 before beginning the project.

1. Prepare a 17" x 18" piece of silk and stretch it onto the frame. Prepare the pattern.

2. Depending on the thickness of the silk, apply 1 to 2 coats of Deka Silk stop-flow primer. Use the 1"-wide foam brush and overlapping strokes to apply the primer.

3. Trace the pattern lightly onto the silk with a pencil.

4. Paint the stripes in the tablecloth cherry.

5. Mixing water and royal blue paint, paint the background and one fish a medium blue.

6. Paint the cat's eyes and the mat under the fish bowl buttercup yellow.

7. Dilute chestnut brown paint with water to paint the cat. I added a small amount of cinnamon to the diluted mixture to create color variations on the paws and ears.

8. Paint the lighter grass mint green.

9. Paint the area behind the grass with a mix of buttercup yellow and a tiny amount of mint green.

10. Paint the darker sea grass leaves with a mixture of royal blue and mint green.

11. Paint the orange fish first with buttercup yellow and add tiny amounts of cherry while the yellow paint is still wet.

12. The yellow fish is painted with the mix of buttercup yellow and mint green from step 9.

13. Paint the cat's pupils ebony.

14. Cure, heat-set, and press the silk as described in "Heat Setting and Care of Painted Silk" on page 18.

Free-Motion Embroidery and Quilting

1. Cut a piece of muslin and a piece of batting the same size as the painted fabric. Baste the fabrics together with pins or basting spray. Place the muslin on the bottom, the batting in the middle, and the painted silk on top, right side facing up.

2. Referring to "To Hoop or Not to Hoop" on page 25, place the center of the design in your embroidery hoop, attach a darning foot, and thread the sewing-machine needle with light tan thread.

3. Fill in areas around eyes and muzzle with the light tan thread.

4. Fill in the cat's pupils and the outline of the eyes, nose, and mouth with black thread. Stitch the fish eyes with black thread, too.

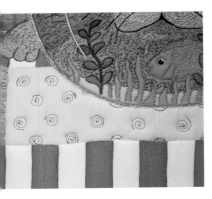

Decorate the tablecloth with freehand spirals in a random pattern.

Attach seed beads by hand to add dimension.

5. Stitch the lines in the tablecloth, the spirals in the yellow mat, and the details in the yellow and orange fish with red thread.

6. With yellow thread, outline and stitch details on the blue fish. Also use yellow thread to stitch around the mat on the table and create the fringe. Fill in the yellow part of the cat's eyes; then stitch a line of light green thread in the eyes to add color and dimension.

7. Outline the top of the cat's head, ears, whiskers, and paws with dark brown thread. Using light tan and medium brown threads, create additional colors and textures on the cat's face and paws.

8. Create a pattern on the blue background with vertical red stitches and horizontal yellow stitches.

9. Outline the grasses in light and medium green threads.

10. Create the water line near the rim of the fish bowl with turquoise thread. Stitch 2 curved lines in white thread on the front of the bowl to resemble reflecting light.

11. Complete your embroidery with several lines of stitching in metallic silver thread to outline the fish bowl.

12. If you want, you can stitch small, clear seed beads by hand to the eyes of the cat and the fish. Sew additional beads to represent bubbles coming from the mouths of the fish.

Making the Wall Hanging

1. Remove any pins from the fabric, and lightly press from the wrong side. Trim the fabric to 14" x 15½". Stitch along the sides ½" from the edge to create a stitching line to guide you when attaching the border.

2. Cut 2 pieces of gold dupioni silk, each 2¼" x 15". With right sides together, sew the gold borders to the 2 sides of the quilt following the stitching line from step 1. Press the seams away toward the borders.

3. Cut 2 strips of the dupioni, each 2¼" x 16". With right sides together, sew gold silk to the top and the bottom of the quilt using a ½" seam allowance.

4. Cut a piece of muslin or other backing fabric the same size as the finished quilt top, which should be approximately 17" x 18½". With right sides together, stitch the quilt top and the backing together, leaving an opening for turning. Reinforce stitching at the corners and trim them diagonally.

5. Turn the quilt right side out, press lightly, and hand stitch the opening closed.

6. Referring to "Hanging Your Art" on page 28, add a hanging sleeve.

Wall Hanging
Enlarge pattern 200 percent.

CAT AND MOUSE TABLE RUNNER *by Sheila Haynes Rauen, 2000, Knoxville, Tennessee, 14½" x 49". Though these two little guys are running across gingham, they don't have to be limited to a table. They might feel equally at home gracing a wall or even hanging as a banner on a door. You can whip up this project quickly and easily with fusible appliqué; then have fun embellishing your critters with machine embroidery.*

Materials

NOTE: *All fabrics are 42"-wide cotton fabrics, unless otherwise specified.*

- ❀ 1¼ yds. black-and-white cotton gingham with 1" squares
- ❀ ¼ yd. red-and-white cotton gingham with 1" squares
- ❀ Rotary cutter, mat, and ruler
- ❀ Sewing thread
- ❀ Bobbin thread
- ❀ ⅓ yd. solid black fabric for cat
- ❀ Gray cotton fabric scraps for mice, cat's nose, and cat's pads on feet
- ❀ Green cotton fabric scrap for cat's eyes
- ❀ Pattern
- ❀ Tracing paper
- ❀ 1 yd. paper-backed fusible web
- ❀ 1½ yds. quilt batting
- ❀ 1½ yds. muslin
- ❀ Basting spray or long quilting pins
- ❀ Thread in white, gray, green, black, and red for machine embroidery
- ❀ Open-toe presser foot
- ❀ Light chalk pencil
- ❀ Darning foot
- ❀ 1½ yds. backing fabric

Enlarging the Pattern

THE CAT pattern on page 70 will need to be enlarged 200 percent. Since some photocopiers only enlarge to 150 percent, you may need to enlarge the pattern in two steps. First, enlarge the pattern 150 percent. Then take the photocopy of the pattern and place it onto the photocopy machine; enlarge it by 133 percent. You will have to enlarge the pattern in sections and tape the pieces together. Please note that the mice patterns on page 71 do not need to be enlarged.

Assembling the Table Runner

BE SURE to read "Appliqué Techniques for Felt and Cotton" on pages 19–22 and "Embellishing with Free-Motion Embroidery and Quilting" on pages 23–29 before beginning the project.

1. Wash and dry your cotton fabrics, and press them while they're still slightly damp to prevent any dried-in creases.

2. Using the squares in the gingham as a guide, cut 1 piece of the black-and-white fabric 16½" x 42½".

3. For the ends, cut 2 pieces of red-and-white gingham 6" x 17½". Fold the red gingham pieces in half to find their centers, and crease the fold to mark the center. Place a long, rotary-cutting ruler on the red gingham, aligning one end with a bottom corner of the fabric and the other end with the midpoint crease on the opposite side of the fabric. Trim off the corner of the fabric with your rotary cutter. Repeat for the other corner to make an end triangle. Then do the same for the other piece of red gingham.

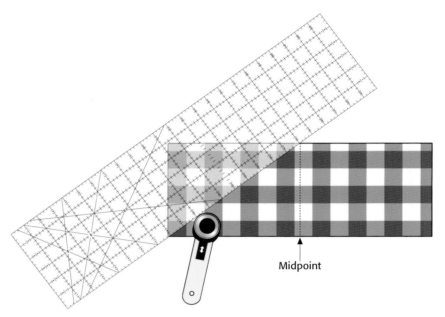

Midpoint

4. Using a ½" seam allowance, sew a red gingham triangle to each end of the black gingham. Press the seams toward the black fabric.

5. Referring to "Appliqué Techniques for Felt and Cotton," prepare your appliqué shapes. Using a tracing paper overlay, fuse the cat's body, head, and tail into position on the black gingham. Fuse the green for the cat's eyes, the gray for the cat's nose, and the gray for the paw pads on the hind paws.

6. Fuse the mice into position, one on each red gingham end triangle and one running in front of the cat.

7. Cut a piece of batting and a piece of muslin the same size as the table runner, which should be 16½" x 52½", and baste the 3 layers together. Place the muslin on the bottom, followed by the batting, and then the table runner with the right side facing up.

Embroidering and Quilting the Table Runner

1. To add detail to the cat and mice, and to make sure they are securely held in place, you'll need to stitch around them. Using a machine or hand blanket stitch, sew around the cat's body, head, and tail with white embroidery thread. If you are sewing by machine, I recommend using an open-toe presser foot.

   NOTE: *Before stitching around the head and tail, outline these sections with a light chalk pencil to help you see where to stitch.*

2. Satin stitch around each mouse with gray thread. Continue the satin stitching behind each mouse to create a tail.

3. Outline the cat's eyes, nose, and the center line of his muzzle with a satin stitch in white thread.

4. Set your machine for a feather stitch or other decorative stitch of your choice and use green thread to stitch along the seams where the red and black fabrics are joined at each end.

5. Using a darning foot and white embroidery thread, create spirals on the cat's body and face. Stitch the whiskers, as well as the detail lines in the ears and mouth. Also with the white thread, stitch details on the cat's front paws and the pads on the back paws.

6. With black thread, outline the inner part of the cat's pupils. Sew lines around the ears of each mouse and stitch tiny spirals to create the eyes and noses of the mice and the shading in their ears.

7. Stitch gray lines to create texture on the ears, heads, and bodies of the mice.

8. With red thread, decorate the gingham background with spiral roses. Use green thread to add stems and leaves.

Finishing the Table Runner

1. Cut the backing fabric the same size and shape as the table runner top. Use your table runner as the pattern.

2. With right sides together, sew the front and back pieces together with a ½" seam allowance. Leave an opening for turning along one of the long straight sides. Reinforce the stitching at the corners, and trim the seams diagonally.

3. Turn the table runner right side out and press. Hand stitch the opening closed.

Use white thread to appliqué the cat so that he shows up well.

Add details to the mice with stitching.

Cat
Enlarge pattern 200 percent
and join halves at dashed line.

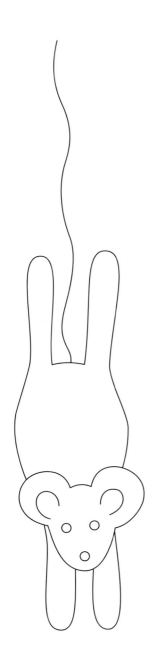

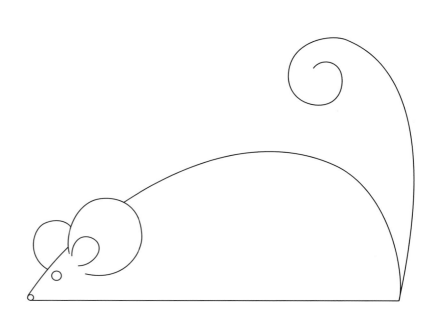

Mice
Do not enlarge patterns.

FELINE FRIEND *Appliquéd Wool-Felt Wall Hanging*

FELINE FRIEND *by Sheila Haynes Rauen, 2000, Knoxville, Tennessee, 14 ½" x 17". My daughter, Julie, occasionally wraps our cat, Gabriel, around her neck like a muffler, but I had to take artistic license in designing this project because Gabriel never looks quite as happy about it as this little guy does! I love the look of wool felt and was enthused by the idea of creating a shaped felt frame to complete this piece. Beads add a final touch and extra dimension that can truly make your work sparkle.*

Materials

NOTE: *Avoid folding the completed project because felt tends to mold itself into the shape you leave it in. You can press the felt to restore the smoothness of the surface, but that can be a little tricky with beads on the surface.*

- ❀ Wool-blend felt from National Nonwovens:
    - 7" x 8" piece of clay or desired skin-tone color for girl's face and neck
    - 7" x 11" piece of dark brown or desired color for girl's hair
    - 5" x 11" piece of barn red for dress
    - 3" x 5" piece of white for collar
    - 7" x 8" piece of copper for cat
    - 12" x 14" piece of relish green for background
    - 2 gold pieces, each 16" x 18", for frame
- ❀ ⅓ yd. muslin
- ❀ Pattern
- ❀ Heat-transfer pen
- ❀ Basting spray or quilting pins
- ❀ Thread in white, dark brown, green, black, red, rose, tan, copper, dark green, metallic gold, and gold for machine embroidery
- ❀ ½ yd. fusible web (Steam-A-Seam 2 works well on wool felt.)
- ❀ Tracing paper
- ❀ Gold and red glass beads
- ❀ Quilting or other heavy thread in desired color for sewing beads to fabric
- ❀ Hand-sewing needle
- ❀ ½ yd. medium- to heavy-weight fusible interfacing
- ❀ Bobbin thread
- ❀ Curtain rings

Enlarging the Pattern

THE PATTERN on page 77 will need to be enlarged 200 percent. Since some photocopiers only enlarge to 150 percent, you may need to enlarge the pattern in two steps. First, enlarge the pattern 150 percent. Then take the photocopy of the pattern and place it onto the photocopy machine; enlarge it by 133 percent. You will have to enlarge the pattern in sections and tape the pieces together.

Making the Girl's Face

BE SURE to read "Appliqué Techniques for Felt and Cotton" on pages 19–22 and "Embellishing with Free-Motion Embroidery and Quilting" on pages 23–29 before beginning the project. When I portray people in fabric projects, I prefer to embroider the face on the fabric with only a thin stabilizer underneath, cut out the face after I've finished the embroidery, and then add it to the background fabric. Otherwise, you can distort the face shape by stitching on it over the layers of fabric and batting.

Embroider the girl's face.

1. Cut 1 piece of clay felt and 1 piece of muslin, 7" x 6", for the girl's face.

2. Prepare the pattern. Trace the outline of the girl's head and the face details in reverse onto a piece of white paper with a heat transfer pen, which is available at fabric shops and craft stores. Following the manufacturer's instructions, place the drawn face, inked side down, onto the right side of the clay felt. Press with an iron to transfer the pattern to your fabric.

3. Spray-baste the muslin or another stabilizer to the wrong side of the felt.

4. Lower the feed dogs on your sewing machine. Using a darning foot and white embroidery thread, fill in the whites of the girl's eyes and teeth.

5. With dark brown embroidery thread, outline her eyes, make the creases above the eyes, make the bottom of the nose, and make the eyebrows.

6. Fill in her eyes with green and black threads.

7. Use red thread for the upper lip and the outline of the teeth. Use rose thread to fill in the lower lip.

Appliquéing the Wall Hanging

1. Using fusible web that can be dry-cleaned (Steam-A-Seam 2), prepare all pattern pieces for fusing: dark brown for hair and bangs (2 pieces), clay for face and neck (2 pieces), barn red for dress (1 piece), white for collar (2 pieces), and copper for cat (3 pieces). You'll also need to cut out the finished girl's face and apply fusible web to it.

2. Cut a 12" x 13" piece of relish green felt for the background. Cut a 12" x 13" piece of muslin and spray baste it to the back of the felt. The borders will be cut out later after the appliqué and embroidery is completed.

3. Make a tracing paper or mylar overlay (see page 20), and use it as a guide to position all shapes and check for fit before fusing them in place. If you're using Steam-A-Seam 2, it has a sticky surface that will allow you to position your pieces and reposition them as needed. The pieces won't shift, however, unless you move them.

4. Fuse the dress first. Then place the neck, collar, and the cat's 2 body sections into position before pressing them to the background with your iron. The cat's body sections are overlapped slightly by the neck piece. The collar overlaps the neck, and the cat's body pieces overlap the collar.

5. Fuse the girl's face in place.

6. Position the hair in place, with the bangs on top of the side hair. Fuse in place.

7. Place the cat's head in position, with the ear overlapping the girl's hair, and fuse.

Embroidering the Wall Hanging

1. Set up your sewing machine for a satin stitch, or tight zigzag, and use tan thread to match the clay felt. Stitch around the lower face and the neck of the girl.

2. With white thread, satin stitch around the collar pieces.

3. Satin stitch the outline of the cat with the copper-colored thread.

4. Switch your machine settings to a straight stitch and lower or cover the feed dogs for free-motion embroidery. Using tan thread, stitch lines of texture in the cat's head and body, and add highlights in the girl's hair.

5. Use dark brown thread to outline the girl's hair and bangs and to add additional texture to them.

6. Stitch around the cat's eyes, ears, nose, mouth, paws, and pads on the paws with dark brown thread.

7. Fill in the cat's eyes with green and black thread.

8. Stitch the white markings on the cat and random stippling lines on the collar with white thread.

9. On the green background, create spiral flowers with red thread. Using dark green thread, stitch a stem and leaves for each red flower on the background. Also stitch stems and leaves randomly on the dress. (You'll add bead flowers to them later.)

10. Using metallic gold thread, create a necklace chain on the girl's neck.

11. With quilting thread or other heavier thread, hand sew red beads to the flower centers on the green background. Hand sew gold beads to the tops of the stems on the dress. Sew 1 red and 2 gold beads to the center of the gold chain to complete the necklace.

12. To add whiskers to the cat, thread a hand-sewing needle with double thread. From the right side of the wall hanging, push the needle in and back out. Tie a double or triple knot and cut the threads so that the whiskers are approximately 1" long.

Use free-motion embroidery on the cat.

Making the Felt Frame

THE WOOL frame is embellished with metallic gold thread to simulate the look of a carved, wooden frame.

Felt frame and machine-embroidery details

1. Cut 2 pieces of gold felt and 1 piece of fusible interfacing in the shape of the frame. Don't cut out the center portion of the frame; the completed appliqué will be attached to the gold fabric.

2. Fuse the interfacing to the wrong side of 1 piece of the gold felt.

3. Pin the 2 pieces of gold felt together, with the interfacing on the inside and the right sides of the felt facing out.

4. Stitch around the entire frame with gold thread and a tight zigzag stitch.

5. Place the appliquéd picture into position on the frame and stitch around it with a machine blanket stitch. If your machine doesn't have a blanket stitch, you can use a featherstitch or do the blanket stitch by hand.

6. Use metallic gold thread to embellish the frame with machine embroidery. Refer to the project photograph for ideas.

7. Sew small curtain rings to the back of the frame for hanging. See page 28 for details.

Wall Hanging
Enlarge pattern 200 percent.

POSY PURR-SE *Appliquéd Wool-Felt Purse*

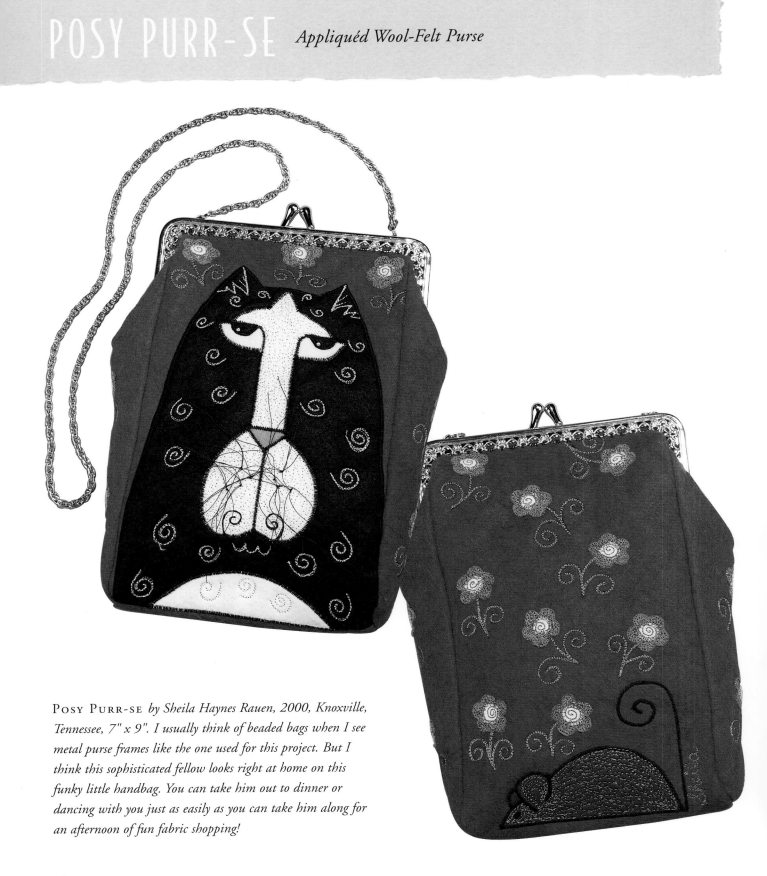

POSY PURR-SE *by Sheila Haynes Rauen, 2000, Knoxville, Tennessee, 7" x 9". I usually think of beaded bags when I see metal purse frames like the one used for this project. But I think this sophisticated fellow looks right at home on this funky little handbag. You can take him out to dinner or dancing with you just as easily as you can take him along for an afternoon of fun fabric shopping!*

Materials

- ❀ Basic pattern for purse (not appliqué), which is included with the frame
- ❀ Heat-transfer pen
- ❀ White paper for pattern
- ❀ Wool-blend felt from National Nonwovens:
    - ½ yd. of barn red
    - scraps of relish green, light yellow, and gray
    - 8" x 6" piece of black
    - 6" x 6" piece of white
    - 4" x 2" piece of brown
- ❀ ½ yd. muslin
- ❀ ½ yd. fusible interfacing (optional)
- ❀ ½ yd. fusible web (Steam-A-Seam 2 works well on felt.)
- ❀ Thread in black, white, tan, green, and red for machine embroidery
- ❀ Hand-sewing needle
- ❀ ½ yd. fabric for lining
- ❀ Brass Purse Frame #BL56, chain of desired length, jump rings, and pliers (all from Bag Lady Press; see "Resources" on page 110)
- ❀ Fabric marking pen or pencil
- ❀ Bobbin thread
- ❀ Sewing thread for purse construction
- ❀ Quilting or other sewing thread for stitching purse to frame

Appliquéing and Embroidering the Fabric

BE SURE to read "Appliqué Techniques for Felt and Cotton" on pages 19–22 and "Embellishing with Free-Motion Embroidery and Quilting" on pages 23–29 before beginning the project. The project patterns are on page 82 and do not need to be enlarged.

1. With a heat transfer pen, trace the 3 pattern pieces for the purse onto white paper. Then, with the transfers face down, press the patterns onto the barn red felt, leaving at least 1" around the marked lines for ease in handling during appliqué and embroidery. Cut the pieces apart, but don't cut out each shape on the drawn lines yet.

2. Fuse muslin or interfacing to the back of each piece of barn red felt to stabilize it. If you're using muslin, fuse the fusible web to it first, and then peel off the paper backing and fuse it to the felt.

3. Cut out and prepare the felt appliqués with fusible web. You'll need the relish green and light yellow felt for flower pieces; the light yellow felt for the cat's eyes; the black, gray, and white felt for the cat; and brown felt for the mouse. Fuse each piece to the background sections of the purse.

4. Satin stitch (tight zigzag stitch) around the cat's head, face details, and chest area with black thread.

5. Satin stitch around the mouse with black thread. Use the same stitch to create the curled tail.

6. Switch your machine settings to a straight stitch and lower or cover the feed dogs for free-motion embroidery. With black embroidery thread, stitch the cat's curved mouth and the mouse's eye.

7. With white thread, sew spirals, ear details, dots in cat's eyes, and texture in the white areas on the cat.

8. Create texture on the mouse with tan thread.

9. With green thread, stitch around the flower petals and create stems and curled leaves.

10. With red thread, sew spirals and feathery lines on the flower centers.

11. To add black whiskers to the cat, thread a hand-sewing needle with black embroidery thread that is doubled. From the right side of the project, push the needle in and back out. Tie a double or triple knot and cut the threads so that the whiskers are approximately 2" long.

Making the Purse

1. Following the manufacturer's directions, cut out the 3 purse pattern pieces from lining fabric. Sew the lining pieces together according to the directions.

2. Cut out the felt purse pieces along the drawn pattern lines. Stitch them together, reinforcing the stitching for extra strength.

3. Sew the lining to the purse according to the manufacturer's directions.

4. Thread a hand-sewing needle with quilting or sewing thread in red or black. As described in the manufacturer's directions, line up the purse with the frame on one side, matching the centers. Sew the edge of the purse to the frame, starting at the center and working your way to the end of the frame on one side. Stitch back to the center, creating a double line of stitching for durability.

5. Repeat step 4, stitching from the center to the other side and back.

Sew the lining to the purse.

6. Sew the other edge of the purse to the other side of the frame as described in steps 4 and 5.

    NOTE: *There will be a gap on each side piece where the fabric is not attached. This is common on many purses and allows for ease when you open the purse.*

7. Decide if you want a shoulder bag or a hand bag, and cut the chain to the desired length. The chain on the purse shown is 28" long.

8. Using the pliers to open the jump rings, attach them to the purse and the chain at each side. Close the rings securely with the pliers.

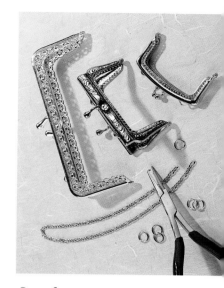

Purse frames come in many shapes and sizes. The chain and hardware are more easily attached with special pliers, but needle-nose pliers will also work.

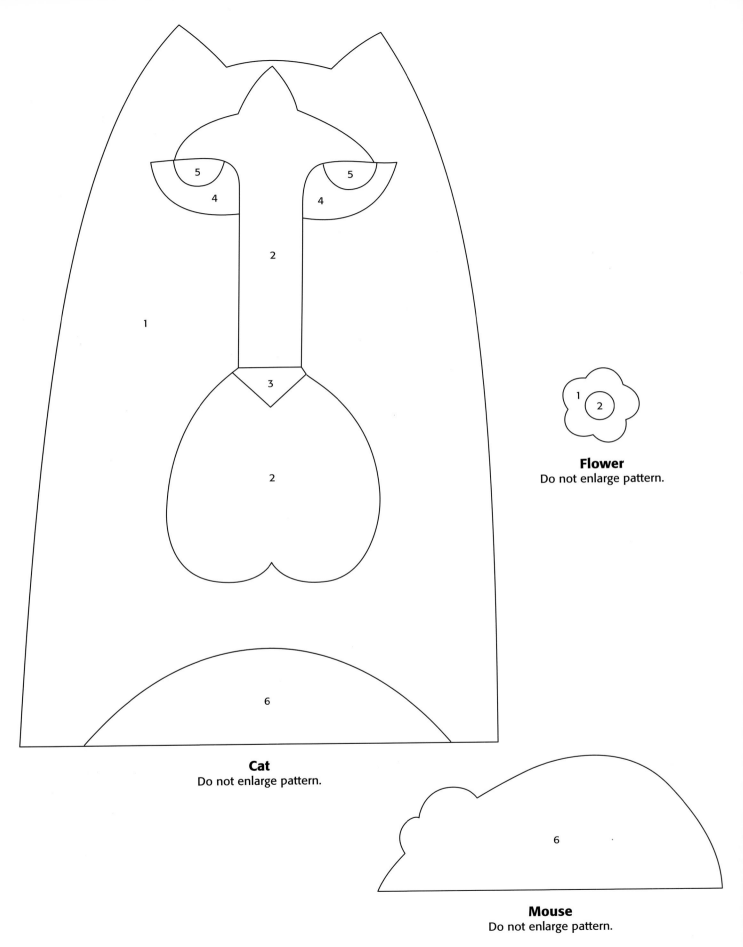

Flower
Do not enlarge pattern.

Cat
Do not enlarge pattern.

Mouse
Do not enlarge pattern.

WATCH YOUR STEP! *Painted Floor Cloth*

WATCH YOUR STEP! *by Sheila Haynes Rauen, 1999, Knoxville, Tennessee, 30" x 39". This black cat epitomizes contentment and satisfaction for his life situation. His only concern is to do just enough to keep his humans happy so that they will pamper him and continue to meet his every need.*

Materials

- 30" x 39" piece of Kunin's Kreative Kanvas Floor Cloth, precut, or other canvas
- Gesso
- 2" flat brush for gesso
- Pattern
- Graphite or other transfer paper
- Soft lead pencil
- Deka Sign Enamel water-based paints in light blue, black, ivory, bright red, emerald green, lemon yellow, and medium gray
- Containers for water and to mix or dilute paints
- Assorted sizes of flat and round brushes
- Flower stamp
- 1"-wide foam brush
- Deka Sign Enamel Clear Coat
- No-skid rug mat, smaller than finished size of floor cloth

Enlarging the Pattern

THE FLOOR cloth pattern on page 86 will need to be enlarged 400 percent. Since some photocopiers only enlarge to 150 percent, you may need to enlarge the pattern in four steps. First, enlarge the pattern 150 percent. Place the photocopy of the pattern onto the photocopy machine; enlarge it by 150 percent. Place this photocopy on the copier and enlarge it 150 percent. Finally, enlarge the last photocopy 118.5 percent. You will have to enlarge the pattern in sections and tape the pieces together.

Painting the Floor Cloth

BE SURE to read "Creating a Floor Cloth" on pages 29–33 before beginning the project. Let each color of paint dry to the touch before adding another color so you won't smear the colors as you work.

1. To make rounded corners like the floor cloth shown, use a dinner plate as a template to draw the curve on each corner of your canvas. Following your marked lines, cut away the corners.

2. Using the 2" flat brush, prime the canvas with gesso on both sides. Prepare the pattern. After the gesso has dried, transfer the pattern to the right side of the canvas with the graphite or transfer paper and a pencil.

3. Stir the paint thoroughly and apply light blue paint to the background. Cover the entire background around the cat. The flowers will be added later, on top of the light blue once it has dried.

4. Paint the cat black and his eyes lemon yellow and black.

5. Paint the fish skeleton with ivory paint.

6. Using the 1"-wide foam brush, apply bright red paint in an even coat to the surface of the flower stamp. Stamp flowers on the light blue background in a random pattern. Reload the stamp with paint after stamping each flower so that you get full coverage of the bright red paint over the blue background.

7. Paint the flower stems and leaves with emerald green paint. Add flower centers with lemon yellow paint.

8. Paint the cat's nose and paw pads medium gray. Add water to the medium gray paint and use a round liner brush to paint outlines and details on the cat's eyes, nose, mouth, whiskers, legs, and fur.

9. Following the manufacturer's instructions, allow the paint to dry completely (4 to 8 hours). Turn the floor cloth over and paint a rim of the light blue background paint to the wrong side for a neat finished edge.

10. When both sides of the floor cloth are dry, apply 3 coats of Deka Sign Enamel Clear Coat finish to the floor cloth. Allow each coat to dry thoroughly before applying the next coat, following the guidelines on the container.

11. Allow the paint to cure for 1 week before using the floor cloth. Then cut a piece of no-skid rug matting 1" smaller all around than the dimensions of the floor cloth. Place the mat underneath the floor cloth before using.

12. Follow directions under "Finishing Touches" on page 32 for taking care of your floor cloth.

Cat face and background flowers

Floor Cloth
Enlarge pattern 400 percent.

MEOW BOX   *Painted Canvas Mailbox Cover*

MEOW BOX *by Sheila Haynes Rauen, 2000, Knoxville, Tennessee, 18½" x 21". Do you ever get bored with the same old mailbox? Just imagine how your mail carrier must feel! Why not paint a mailbox cover you can change with the seasons? This design is ideal for spring and summer, and once you've completed it, I'm sure you'll be anxious to try another. Be sure to use a primer and paints that are suitable for use outdoors, such as Deka Sign Enamel primer and paints.*

Materials

- ❀ 21" x 18½" piece of Kunin's Kreative Kanvas (or a size that will fit your mailbox)
- ❀ Deka Sign Enamel primer
- ❀ 2" flat brush
- ❀ Pattern
- ❀ Graphite or other transfer paper
- ❀ Soft lead pencil
- ❀ Deka Sign Enamel paints in sky blue, white, dark green, emerald green, bright red, brown, black, coral, lemon yellow, orange, and medium gray
- ❀ 2", 1", ¾", and ¼" flat brushes
- ❀ Size 10, 6, 4, and 00 liner round brushes
- ❀ Containers for water and to mix or dilute paints
- ❀ Deer Foot Stippler brush
- ❀ Small piece of sea sponge

Enlarging the Pattern

THE MAILBOX cover pattern on pages 91–92 will need to be enlarged 200 percent. Since some photocopiers only enlarge to 150 percent, you may need to enlarge the patterns in two steps. First, enlarge the pattern 150 percent. Then place the photocopy onto the photocopy machine; enlarge it by 133 percent. You will have to enlarge the pattern in sections and tape the pieces together.

Painting the Mailbox Cover

BE SURE to read "Creating a Floor Cloth" on pages 29–33 before beginning the project. The techniques used to create a floor cloth are also used for making a mailbox cover.

1. Measure the length and width of your mailbox with a tape measure. To measure the width, measure from the bottom of one side, up and over the mailbox to the bottom of the other side. Cut the Kreative Kanvas to the proper size.

2. Prime both sides of the canvas with Deka Sign Enamel primer and a 2" flat brush, allowing one side to dry before applying the primer to the other side.

3. Prepare the pattern. Transfer the design to the primed canvas surface with graphite or other transfer paper and a pencil. You may want to repeat the cat and bird design on both sides or simply paint some hills and a flower on the side with the flag as I have done.

4. Paint the background sky blue and the clouds white.

5. Paint the hill behind the cat dark green, with emerald green, triangular-shaped trees for texture and depth.

6. Paint bright red dots on the trees and give each tree a brown trunk.

7. Paint the hill to the left of the cat medium green and the hill to the right emerald green.

8. Paint the cat black and the areas on his face and his paws white.

9. Paint the cat's nose with coral paint, or create a pink color with white and a tiny amount of bright red paint.

10. Paint the cat's eyes lemon yellow and black.

11. Dilute a small amount of white paint with water for details on the cat's ears, around the eyes, the highlights in the eyes, and the lines in the fur.

12. Paint the sunflower petals lemon yellow, adding tiny amounts of bright red paint into some of the strokes.

13. Paint the sunflower centers lemon yellow.

14. With the Deer Foot Stippler brush, add texture to the sunflower centers by dabbing alternating layers of orange, brown, and lemon yellow paint.

15. Paint the bird bright red, and add white dots when the red paint has dried.

16. Paint the bird's beak and feet orange with orange paint, or mix bright red and lemon yellow to make your own orange paint.

17. Paint details in the wings, feathers, eye, and beak with diluted white paint.

18. Dilute a small amount of medium gray with water to paint the details on the cat's paws and the outline of the nose, mouth, and whiskers.

19. Mix emerald green and lemon yellow for the sunflower stems and leaves.

20. Use diluted dark green paint for shading on the stems and for lines in the leaves. With the Deer Foot Stippler brush or a small sea sponge, dab diluted dark green on the right hill to create shading and texture.

21. Dab diluted lighter green paint, which you mixed for the flower stems and leaves in step 19, on the other 2 hills in the same manner.

22. Paint small dots of sky blue and bright red on the left hill, and white and lemon yellow dots on the right hill with a small round brush.

23. Mix small amounts of emerald green and white paint. Dilute the mixture and use it to paint the blades of grass. Using a round brush, start at the bottom of the canvas and pull upward with the brush, overlapping the background elements.

Cat's face and paws

Bird and sunflower

24. Repeat the same techniques for the opposite side of the mailbox cover. Allow the paint to cure for 1 week before using the mailbox cover. There is no need to add a clear coat, however, since you've used sign enamel paints that are suitable for outdoor use.

Installing the Mailbox Cover

INSTALLATION OF the cover depends on how your mailbox is mounted. You may decide to punch holes or make small X cuts to fit a screw through the cover and into the holes on the bottom of the mailbox in two or three places. Another option is to thread fishing line through the holes and tie the cover securely to the mailbox. Trim the mailbox cover where the door is hinged so that it won't catch on it when opening and closing the door. Cut out a space for the flag, making a template for this with tracing paper beforehand.

Store the mailbox cover flat when it's not being used. Just as with floor cloths, avoid folding or creasing the cover to prevent cracks.

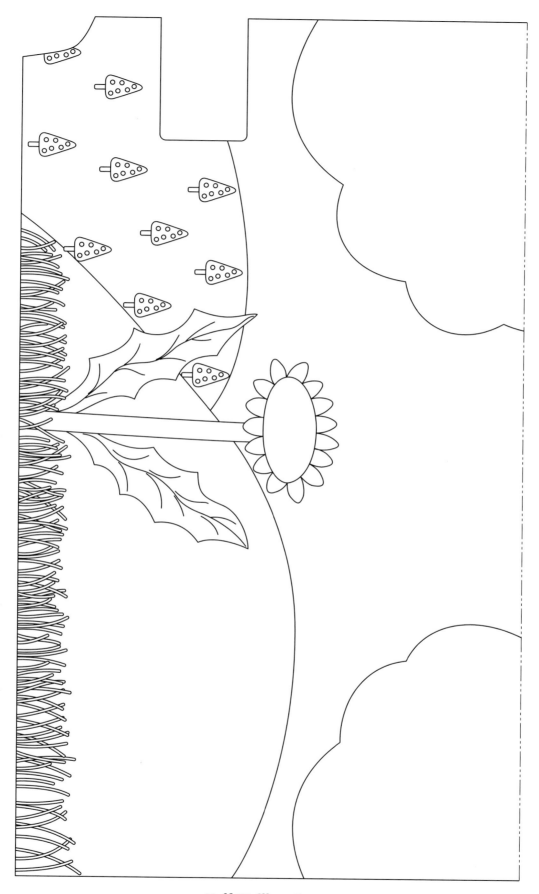

Half Mailbox Cover
Enlarge pattern 200 percent and join halves at dashed line.

Half Mailbox Cover
Enlarge pattern 200 percent and join halves at dashed line.

NICE KITTY

Painted Flowerpot and Birdbath

NICE KITTY *by Sheila Haynes Rauen, 2000, Knoxville, Tennessee, 12¼" (height) x 8" (diameter). Azalea pots are just the right scale to use to create this flowerpot kitty. And I love the option of using this design as a birdbath, too, just by adding a painted clay saucer to the top. I promise, this cat is the friendly type. He can't possibly harm the birds that will most certainly come a-calling.*

If you don't mind investing a bit more time and money in the project, buy larger pots and enlarge the pattern at a copy center to fit your pot. As with any projects made with clay pots, they are meant to be used in the warmer months of the year only. If you expect a frost or freeze, keep them inside to avoid cracking or breaking.

Materials

- ❀ Two 8" azalea pots
- ❀ One 12¼" waterproof clay saucer
- ❀ Sandpaper
- ❀ Deka Sign Enamel primer
- ❀ Pattern
- ❀ Graphite or transfer paper
- ❀ Soft lead pencil
- ❀ Deka Sign Enamel paints in aqua, sky blue, medium gray, lemon yellow, deep magenta, white, black, emerald green, light blue, and violet
- ❀ Assorted sizes of flat and round brushes, including ½" and ¾" flat brushes and a 1" foam brush
- ❀ Containers for water and to mix or dilute paints
- ❀ Glue suitable for outdoor use, such as E-600 or hot gluesticks

Enlarging the Pattern

THE CAT body and tail pattern on page 97 will need to be enlarged 200 percent. Since some photocopiers only enlarge to 150 percent, you may need to enlarge the pattern in two steps. First, enlarge the pattern 150 percent. Then place the photocopy onto the photocopy machine; enlarge it by 133 percent. You will have to enlarge the pattern in sections and tape the pieces together. Please note that the flower, fish, and cat head patterns on page 96 do not need to be enlarged.

Painting the Flowerpot and Birdbath

BE SURE to read "Creating a Floor Cloth" on pages 29–33 before beginning the project. Even though this project is made of clay, you use the same paints and techniques that you use for canvas that will be outdoors, such as the mailbox cover "Meow Box" on page 87.

Paint the fish different colors.

1. Sand any rough areas on the clay pots and saucer, and wipe off the dust.

2. With a 1"-wide foam brush, apply 1 coat of Deka Sign Enamel primer to the outsides of the pots and the saucer. (You don't have to prime the clay, but it will give you a nice light-colored background for the pastel colors used in this project.) Do not paint the insides of the pots or saucer.

3. Prepare the pattern. Transfer the pattern to the clay pots with graphite or other transfer paper and a pencil.

4. Paint the rim of the upper pot aqua, but leave the fish unpainted so that the white of the primer is still showing.

5. Paint the background on the top and the bottom pots sky blue.

6. Paint the cat medium gray.

7. Paint the cat's eyes lemon yellow and black.

8. Paint the fish different colors, as desired. Vary the colors and markings to decorate the fish. Paint black dots for the eyes of the fish.

9. Use white paint to paint the white areas on the cat's face and body, and the details on the cat.

10. Paint the cat's nose black; then outline the cat's eyes, nose, whiskers, and mouth with black paint that has been thinned slightly with water.

11. Mix black paint with a small amount of white to make dark gray paint. Thin the mixture with water to paint shading on the cat and the dark lines in the fur, the paws, and the shading on the muzzle.

12. Paint swirls of deep magenta to create the center area of the flowers, and paint dots of lemon yellow for the flower petals.

13. Use emerald green paint to add stems and leaves to the flowers. Dilute a small amount of emerald green paint and make upward strokes with a round brush to create the grass.

14. Paint the outside rim of the saucer white. When it is dry, use a ¾" flat brush to paint a sky blue checkerboard design around the lower rim of saucer. Use the width of the brush as a guide for placement.

15. With a ½" flat brush, paint an aqua checkerboard design around the upper rim of the saucer. Use the width of the brush as a guide.

16. Paint alternating dots of lemon yellow and deep magenta around the rim of the saucer between the 2 lines of checkerboard designs.

Assembling the Flowerpot or Birdbath

STACK THE 2 pots together. Use an outdoor glue to hold them together. If you are using the saucer to make a birdbath, you may not want to glue the saucer in place because it will be easier to clean and fill it if it's removable. And the weight of the water should hold the saucer in place. If you're going to use your project as a flowerpot, put a layer of pebbles in the bottom of the upper pot before planting anything to provide drainage for your plants.

Cat's face and body

Flowers and grass

Fish
Do not enlarge pattern.

Flower
Do not enlarge pattern.

Align with base of pot.

Cat Head
Do not enlarge pattern.

Cat Body and Tail
Enlarge pattern 200 percent.

Align with base of pot.

CAT CROSSING   *Painted Wood Garden Sign*

CAT CROSSING
*by Sheila Haynes Rauen,
2000, Knoxville, Tennessee,
17½" x 10½". What a
delightful crossing these
cats provide for their fine-
feathered friends. They must
have incredible muscle tone
in their ears to be able to
hold the weight of the birds
as they tiptoe along their
way. And look how well-
behaved these furry felines
are—not an exposed claw or
bared tooth in the bunch!
Use this design indoors or
out—wherever you want to
see folks smile.*

Materials

- ❀ 10½" x 17½" piece of ½"- or ¾"-thick marine or pressure-treated plywood
- ❀ Sandpaper
- ❀ Dust cloth
- ❀ Deka Sign Enamel primer
- ❀ Pattern
- ❀ Graphite or other transfer paper
- ❀ Soft lead pencil
- ❀ Deka Sign Enamel paints in process blue, white, lemon yellow, medium green, medium gray, black, emerald green, ivory, orange, and deep magenta
- ❀ Assorted sizes of flat and round brushes
- ❀ Deer Foot Stippler brush
- ❀ Sea sponge
- ❀ Container for water and for mixing colors and diluting paint
- ❀ Decorative screws and chain
- ❀ Shepherd's crook pole or stake

Enlarging the Pattern

THE SIGN pattern on page 102 will need to be enlarged 200 percent. Since some photocopiers only enlarge to 150 percent, you may need to enlarge the pattern in two steps. First, enlarge the pattern 150 percent. Then take the photocopy of the pattern and place it onto the photocopy machine; enlarge it by 133 percent. You will have to enlarge the pattern in sections and tape the pieces together.

Painting the Sign

BE SURE to read "Painting Wood" on pages 33–34 before beginning the project.

1. Sand the wood and wipe off the dust with a clean, dry cloth. Apply 1 coat of primer meant for outdoor use.

2. Prepare the pattern. Transfer the design to primed surface with graphite or transfer paper and a pencil.

3. Paint the back of the sign and the background of the front side with process blue paint.

   NOTE: *For each color on the front of the sign, let it wrap around to the narrow edge of the wood for a professional look.*

4. Paint the cloud white and the sun lemon yellow.

Gray cat

Tabby cat

Black cat

5. Paint the hills medium green.

6. Paint the left cat medium gray and white. Paint his nose black.

7. Paint the gray cat's eyes lemon yellow mixed with a small amount of emerald green.

8. Paint the middle tabby cat ivory, white, and dark orange. Dark orange is made by mixing brown with orange.

9. Paint the tabby cat's eyes lemon yellow with a small amount of deep magenta.

10. Paint the right cat black and white.

11. Paint the black cat's nose pink by mixing white and deep magenta. Paint his eyes light blue by mixing white and process blue. Add a curved line in the light blue of the cat's eye with a stroke of process blue paint that you've thinned with water.

12. Paint one bird deep magenta and the other lemon yellow. Paint the bird's beaks, legs, and feet orange. Paint the bird's eyes and the darks of the cats' eyes black.

13. Mix a small amount of lemon yellow and deep magenta, and dilute the mixture with water to create a wash to paint the center of the sun. You can also apply this wash very lightly to the yellow bird for shading.

14. Dilute white paint with water. Dip the Deer Foot Stippler brush into the paint and dab off the excess paint onto a paper towel. Very lightly dab the brush onto the gray cat to create a subtle texture. Use the same white wash and a small brush to create the lighter tones on the black cat's muzzle and on each side of his head.

15. Paint a black outline around the eyes, nose, and mouth of the gray cat.

16. Dilute a mix of black and medium gray paint to make the shadows under the gray cat's eyes, on each side of the nose and muzzle, and under the mouth. Use the same mixture to paint the whiskers and the detail on the ears, and to paint under the black cat's eyes and on each side of the black cat's nose.

17. Dilute a small amount of medium gray paint to use for the mouth, fur, and ears on the black cat.

18. Paint the tabby cat's nose brown; then dilute a small amount of brown paint to outline the tabby cat's eyes, ears, mouth, and whiskers.

19. Thin the same brown from step 18 even further to make a wash to add shading under the tabby cat's eyes, along the nose, and around the cat's muzzle. Use the same wash to paint detail lines in the fur and the shading in the eyes.

20. Paint dots of emerald green on the deep magenta bird.

21. Paint darker lines on the wings and feathers of the deep magenta bird by mixing deep magenta and brown, which is then thinned with water. Use the same mix to shade the lower part of the birds' beaks.

22. Paint dots on the lemon yellow bird and the line around the bird's eye with process blue. Dilute the process blue to paint the feather lines on the bird.

23. Create texture on the hills by dabbing small amounts of a mixture of emerald green and white paints. Use a sea sponge or the Deer Foot Stippler brush to apply the paint.

24. Paint small dots of deep magenta, lemon yellow, and light blue (a mix of process blue and white) to create flowers on the hills.

Completing the Sign

1. Install cup hook screws at each end of the top of the sign.

2. Hook chain of the desired length onto the screws. Make sure your chain is suitable for outdoor use and won't rust.

3. Hang the sign on a shepherd's crook pole as shown, or as desired.

Garden Sign
Enlarge pattern 200 percent.

PLATTER PUSS *Painted Glass Platter*

PLATTER PUSS *by Sheila Haynes Rauen, 2000, Knoxville, Tennessee, 14" diameter. This platter will add a touch of whimsy and color to your collection of serving pieces. Children are especially delighted to discover this charming fellow under glass once all the cookies are gobbled up! If you've never tried glass painting before, don't be hesitant. It's quick and easy to do, and today's paints are better than ever.*

Materials

- ❧ 14" diameter glass platter, such as Anchor Hocking
- ❧ Pattern
- ❧ Tape
- ❧ China marker (optional)
- ❧ Pébéo Vitrea 160 glass paints in black outliner, earth brown, oriental green, sun yellow, pepper red, amaranthine (violet), turquoise, lazuli, and ink black
- ❧ Assorted sizes of round and flat brushes with soft bristles
- ❧ Household oven

Painting the Platter

READ "Painting Glass and Ceramics" on page 34 before beginning the project. The project patterns are on page 105 and do not need to be enlarged.

1. Wash and dry the glass platter, and prepare the pattern.

2. Tape the patterns *face down* on the top of the plate. You can either leave it in place as a pattern to paint by, or trace the design directly onto the bottom of the glass with a china marker.

3. Outline the cat and fish with the black outliner paint.

4. Using a round brush and downward strokes, paint the cat earth brown.

5. Paint the cat's eyes oriental green and the pupils ink black.

6. Paint the fish in a variety of colors and patterns. Experiment with layering colors as well as mixing colors right on the glass.

7. Paint wavy lines with lazuli and oriental green on the rim of the platter.

8. Allow the paint to dry thoroughly before you heat-set the paints in the oven. Follow the manufacturer's directions for this process, as well as for cleaning and maintaining the look of your painted glassware.

Center of plate

Fish swimming along rim

Cat
Do not enlarge pattern.

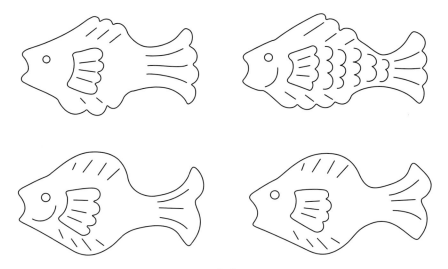

Fish
Do not enlarge patterns.

MOUSE AND COOKIES

Painted Ceramic Mug and Plate

MOUSE AND COOKIES *by Sheila Haynes Rauen, 2000, Knoxville, Tennessee, 3½" mug and 8"-diameter plate. Painting this design on a mug and plate would make a purr-fect gift for a child or for a cat lover of any age. If you are very industrious, you may want to paint a whole set to use at your next "catnip" tea party.*

Materials

- ❀ Light yellow mug and plate from Newcor (available at home improvement stores in many colors)
- ❀ Graphite paper or Pébéo transfer paper
- ❀ Soft lead pencil
- ❀ ⅜"-wide flat brush for checkerboard design, and small round brushes in 2 or 3 sizes
- ❀ Pébéo Porcelaine 150 paints in scarlet red, olivine green, abyss black, light scale brown, ivory, havana brown, marseille yellow, and oriental green
- ❀ Tracing paper for pattern
- ❀ Household oven

Painting the Mug and Plate

BE SURE to read "Painting Glass and Ceramics" on page 34 before beginning the project. The pattern for this project is on page 108 and does not need to be enlarged.

1. Wash and dry mug and plate.

2. Prepare the pattern by tracing it onto tracing paper. Transfer the pattern lightly to the surface of the mug and plate with graphite paper or transfer paper and pencil.

3. Using the width of the ⅜" brush as a guide, paint a checkerboard design around the rim of the plate and the bottom of the mug in scarlet red.

4. Paint the cat's eyes olivine green.

5. Outline the cat's eyes and paint the dark part of the eyes abyss black.

6. Using a small round brush, paint the cat's body light scale brown and ivory. Refer to the photograph for guidance. Add shading and outlines to the cat with havana brown.

7. Mix ivory and abyss black to make gray paint for the mouse. Paint darker areas on the mouse with a darker gray mixture.

8. Paint the mouse's eye, nose, tail, and feet abyss black.

9. Paint flowers in a scattered pattern on the mug and along the border of the plate. Use scarlet red for the petals, marseille yellow for the flower centers, and oriental green for the stems and leaves.

10. Paint ivory dots between the flowers to complete the painting.

Mug

Plate

11. Allow the paint to dry thoroughly before heat setting the plate and mug in the oven. Follow the manufacturer's directions for this process, as well as for cleaning and maintenance of your painted ceramics.

Mug
Do not enlarge pattern.

AFTERWORD

I AM CONVINCED that each of us has an incredible potential for creative expression. Most of what we need is already part of us. We just have to learn to listen to ourselves and ignore the negativity that we all deal with from time to time. I hope you have been inspired to trust yourself and try new things. You will learn something new from everything you do—one creative experience will lead to another.

I am reminded of something my second-grade teacher used to say over and over again—"*I can't* means *I won't.*" This must have really made an impression on me, because I still remember it after such a long time. I think this saying is a good thing for adults to hear and remember as well. It's time to start saying "I can!" Best of luck to you!

Arty's
Janlynn Corporation
34 Front Street
PO Box 51848
Indian Orchard, MA 01151-5848
1-800-445-5565
www.janlynn.com
Silks, silk blanks, frames

Bag Lady Press
PO Box 2409
Evergreen, CO 80437-2409
1-888-222-4523
www.baglady.com
Purse frames, chains, pliers

Bernina of America
3500 Thayer Court
Aurora, IL 60504
1-630-978-2500
www.berninausa.com
Sewing machines

Deka Paints
Box 309 Lamoille Industrial Park
Morrisville, VT 05661
1-800-532-7895
Silk paints, Deka Sign Enamel

Dharma Trading Company
PO Box 150916
San Rafael, CA 94915
1-800-542-5227
Silk, silk blanks, silk and fabric painting supplies, Milsoft fabric softener

Fairfield Processing Corporation
PO Box 1130
Danbury, CT 06813
1-800-243-0989
www.poly-fil.com
Quilt battings, stuffings, pillow forms

JoAnn Stores, Inc.
5555 Darrow Rd.
Hudson, OH 44236
1-330-656-2600
Garden Gate 4' shepherd's crook

Kunin Felt
A Foss Manufacturing Company
380 Lafayette Road
PO Box 5000
Hampton, NH 03843-5000
1-603-929-6100
www.kuninfelt.com
Kreative Kanvas

Loew-Cornell Brushes
563 Chestnut Avenue
Teaneck, NJ 07666-2490
1-201-836-7070
Paint brushes, Deer Foot Stippler brush, Paint Eraser Tool

National Nonwovens
PO Box 150
Easthampton, MA 01027
1-800-333-3469
1-413-527-3445
www.nationalnonwovens.com
Wool-blend felts

Ott-Light Technology
1214 W. Cass St.
Tampa, FL 33606
1-813-621-0058
True-color Ott Lights: floor, desk, and clamp-on models

Pébéo of America, Inc.
PO Box 717
Swanton, VT 05488
1-819-829-5012
www.pebeo.com
Glass and ceramic paints, transfer paper

Sulky of America
3113 Broadpoint Drive
Harbor Heights, FL 33983
www.sulky.com
Decorative threads, stabilizers, basting spray

Timid Thimble Creations
14298 Esprit Drive
Westfield, IN 46074
1-317-818-9469
www.timidthimble.com
Quilter's Gloves by Nancy Odom

The Warm Company
954 East Union Street
Seattle, WA 98122
1-800-234-WARM
www.warmcompany.com
Steam-A-Seam 2 double-stick, iron-on fusible web

YLI Corporation
161 West Main Street
Rock Hill, SC 29730
www.ylicorp.com
e-mail: ylicorp@rhtc.net
Decorative threads, ribbons, bobbin threads

Sheila Haynes Rauen has been drawing, painting, and sewing for as long as she can remember. While pursuing her Fine Arts studies at the Uni-versity of Tennessee, she felt she was home at last. The years of studying art history, drawing, painting, and sculpting led her to develop her own personal style and a love for working in a variety of mediums.

When an executive with an art manufacturing company saw her work, she began a new phase in her career. For several years she has been designing and creating projects for many popular magazines, demonstrating at trade shows, and appearing on a variety of television programs. Sheila is a frequent guest on the HGTV television program *The Carol Duvall Show*. She also works with several craft product manufacturers.

Sheila is currently focusing on creating art quilts and dolls. She feels that the many skills she has developed over the years are coming together in new and exciting ways. She says, "I am so blessed to be doing what I love!"

Sheila and her husband live in Knoxville, Tennessee. They have two daughters, and the whole family is owned by two cats—Natty and Gabriel.

NEW AND BESTSELLING TITLES FROM

America's Best-Loved Craft & Hobby Books™

America's Best-Loved Quilt Books®

QUILTING
From That Patchwork Place, an imprint of Martingale & Company

Appliqué
Artful Appliqué
Colonial Appliqué
Red and Green: An Appliqué Tradition
Rose Sampler Supreme
Your Family Heritage: Projects in
    Appliqué

Baby Quilts
Appliqué for Baby
The Quilted Nursery
Quilts for Baby: Easy as ABC
More Quilts for Baby: Easy as ABC
Even More Quilts for Baby: Easy as ABC

Holiday Quilts
Easy and Fun Christmas Quilts
Favorite Christmas Quilts from That
    Patchwork Place
Paper Piece a Merry Christmas
A Snowman's Family Album Quilt
Welcome to the North Pole

Learning to Quilt
Basic Quiltmaking Techniques for:
    Borders and Bindings
    Curved Piecing
    Divided Circles
    Eight-Pointed Stars
    Hand Appliqué
    Machine Appliqué
    Strip Piecing
The Joy of Quilting
The Quilter's Handbook
Your First Quilt Book (or it should be!)

Paper Piecing
50 Fabulous Paper-Pieced Stars
A Quilter's Ark
Easy Machine Paper Piecing
Needles and Notions
Paper-Pieced Curves
Show Me How to Paper Piece

Rotary Cutting
101 Fabulous Rotary-Cut Quilts
365 Quilt Blocks a Year Perpetual
    Calendar
Fat Quarter Quilts
Lap Quilting Lives!
Quick Watercolor Quilts
Quilts from Aunt Amy
Spectacular Scraps
Time-Crunch Quilts

Small & Miniature Quilts
Bunnies By The Bay Meets Little Quilts
Celebrate! with Little Quilts
Easy Paper-Pieced Miniatures
Little Quilts All Through the House

CRAFTS
From Martingale & Company

300 Papermaking Recipes
The Art of Handmade Paper and
    Collage
The Art of Stenciling
Creepy Crafty Halloween
Gorgeous Paper Gifts
Grow Your Own Paper
Stamp with Style
Wedding Ribbonry

KNITTING
From Martingale & Company

Comforts of Home
Fair Isle Sweaters Simplified
Knit It Your Way
Simply Beautiful Sweaters
Two Sticks and a String
The Ultimate Knitter's Guide
Welcome Home: Kaffe Fassett

COLLECTOR'S COMPASS™
From Martingale & Company

20th Century Glass
'50s Decor
Barbie® Doll
Jewelry
20th Century Dinnerware
United States Coins
Movie Collectibles
'60s and '70s Decor

Our books are available at bookstores and your favorite craft, fabric, yarn, and antiques retailers. If you don't see the title you're looking for, visit us at **www.martingale-pub.com** or contact us at:

1-800-426-3126
International: 1-425-483-3313
Fax: 1-425-486-7596
E-mail: info@martingale-pub.com

For more information and a full list of our titles, visit our Web site or call for a free catalog.